Big Ideas in
Small Packages:
Using Picture Books
with Older Readers

Molly Blake Pearson

Linworth
PUBLISHING, INC

Your Trusted
Library-to-Classroom Connecti
Books, Magazines, and Onlin

Library of Congress Cataloging-in-Publication Data

Pearson, Molly Blake.
  Big ideas in small packages : using picture books with older readers /
Molly Blake Pearson.
       p. cm.
  Includes bibliographical references and index.
  ISBN 1-58683-178-X (pbk.)
  1. Picture books for children—Bibliography. 2. Children—Books and
reading. I. Title.
Z1037.A1P39 2005
011.62—dc22

                              2004025782

Published by Linworth Publishing, Inc.
480 East Wilson Bridge Road, Suite L
Worthington, Ohio 43085

Copyright © 2005 by Linworth Publishing, Inc.

ISBN: 1-58683-178-X

5 4 3 2 1

Table of Contents

Introduction

The room is silent. The librarian is reading the picture book *Pink and Say*, by Patricia Polacco, to a group of fifth grade students. Suddenly, a student bursts out, "That's not fair! Why did the soldiers separate Pink from Say at Andersonville? Why did they hang the black prisoners? Did Pink hang?" The discussion that follows leads the class into an impassioned examination of the Civil War. Topics include, the status of black soldiers in the Civil War, the conditions in confederate camps such as Andersonville, and the reasons for and consequences of the war. Students generate provocative questions for further research and plan another visit to the library to gather more information. With a twenty-minute read aloud, the librarian has effectively hooked the students into an in depth study of the Civil War. The power of a single picture book to create interest in a topic is immense.

Picture books are short books, usually 32 to 48 pages long, in which the illustrations and text work together to tell a story or provide information. Parents and educators have long had the perception that picture books are for the very young. While that is certainly true in some cases, many picture books speak to the older reader as well. As a teacher and librarian, I have had the opportunity to use picture books with all ages and have found over the years that many picture books are more suited for older students. One of my passions is to show teachers and students that one does not need to stop reading picture books after third grade. To that end, I began teaching a graduate level distance-learning course on the use of picture books with older readers and, encouraged by the positive response to the class, began thinking about other ways to share this experience with teachers and librarians.

One of the current trends in children's literature is the publication of picture books for a more mature audience. Increasingly, authors are writing books that look like picture books, but are not intended or appropriate for an audience of preschool or early elementary school children. Many of these books are wonderful to use with older readers. It takes time to find the right picture book for a particular unit. My goals with this book are to encourage educators, at all levels, to use these quality picture books with their students and to provide suggestions for appropriate titles to add value to the curriculum.

This book is designed for teachers and librarians of grades four through twelve and can be used with teachers in training. It will help educators choose picture books and integrate them into a unit on a particular subject. Discussion questions and suggested activities for each book will give the teacher or librarian ideas for use beyond a simple read-aloud.

Big Ideas in Small Packages: Using Picture Books with Older Readers begins with a rationale for the use of picture books with older readers. Subsequent chapters contain annotated bibliographies of picture books grouped by subject. The annotations include a summary, discussion questions, and suggested activities for the featured books. Book Link sections include additional books on the topic or by the same author with brief summaries where appropriate. An index of authors and illustrators and a title index are included to aid in the use of this book.

Chapter 1

Why Use Picture Books

with Older Readers?

As parents raise their children, they read many picture books to them, beginning shortly after birth and continuing into elementary school. Many adults stop reading picture books to children by the fourth grade, when the youngsters begin to read chapter books for themselves. Teachers also tend to choose only chapter books for read-aloud beyond fourth grade. While teachers and parents are tempted to think of all picture books as appropriate only for the very young—the preschool through primary age crowd, librarians have long known that picture books have a much wider audience. Picture books, such as Donald Crews's *Freight Train*, are best suited for the younger reader; a joy to share with a child sitting on your lap or read to a group of small children. Many other titles, such as *Patrol: an American Soldier in Vietnam*, by Walter Dean Myers, are clearly unsuitable for younger children. In recent years, picture books have frequently targeted a much wider, older audience. This gives educators a completely new type of picture book to investigate.

Picture books cover many subjects in ways that make the topics accessible to a younger audience, but many may contain content that goes over the heads of younger children. Some picture books are simply not developmentally appropriate or useful at grades PreK-2 because of subject matter, word choice, or conceptual level. That is not to say these books cannot or should not be used in the primary grades, but for many of the books, the story, the humor, the message, or the subject matter may be lost on the younger students. As every book has its intended audience, every book also has its best, most suited audience, where the book works fully.

While it is difficult to categorize many books, picture books for older readers can fit loosely into several categories. First, there are books with more advanced humor. Jon Scieszka's *True Story of the Three Pigs* is a good example. While first graders enjoy the story, older children, up through middle and high school, can learn much about parody and truly get all the jokes intended by the author and illustrator. At the very least, the fractured fairy tale genre requires from its audience a solid grounding in the classic fairy tales, which younger children are only beginning to develop. To the child who does not know traditional versions of the *Three Little Pigs*, the *True Story of the Three Pigs* is fun as a stand alone, but the reader who has prior experience with many fairy tales will truly appreciate all the humor in the pictures and the words of the parody. Similarly, a more advanced reader best understands puns and other word play. While younger children enjoy the basic story of *The Library Dragon*, by Carmen Agra Deedy, some of the word play is lost on them. For instance, the library dragon's name is Miss Lotta Scales. Often, the illustrator has adds to the humor of a book with visual puns, signs in the pictures, even illustrations that carry the story farther than the text.

Historical vignettes are another category of picture books that are useful for older readers. Picture books can tell difficult stories about the human cost of war, the heroic and horrific acts of humankind, and the sad and moving personal tales that make history more real to the reader in a strikingly visual format. In 32 evocatively illustrated pages, an author can move us to tears and, in the process, spark an interest in finding out more. What better way for high school students to understand the achingly difficult decisions people have had to make in wartime than to hear or read *The Faithful Elephants*, by Yukio Tsuchiya, the story of the heart-wrenching decisions made about the animals in the zoo when Tokyo was in danger of being bombed in World War II. To prevent wild animals from creating additional havoc by escaping into a bombed city, officials decide to euthanize the zoo's residents. After all other available methods fail to put the elephants to sleep, zookeepers have no choice but to starve the unfortunate creatures to death. The book clearly illustrates the anxiety and grief of the people at the zoo and in Tokyo over the consequences of a decision intended to protect the citizens of the city. If you read this book to an adult audience, you will see tears. A second grader does not have the prior knowledge or maturity to understand this story, but as high school students study World War II, stories like this add to their knowledge and make history come alive. The magic is that a teacher can accomplish so much with a 20 minute read aloud. Armed with a careful selection of picture books that coordinate with the instructional curriculum, a high school or middle school teacher or librarian can breathe life into, what many teenagers will tell you, is "dry, boring, history."

Picture books can effectively introduce many science concepts. Inquiry methods of science demand a hands-on approach, and the literature in picture books can provide a wonderful opportunity for creating questions to investigate further. *Snowflake Bentley*, by Jacqueline Briggs Martin, is an example of a book that works as part of a unit on weather or snow with older children. The story of the discovery that no two snowflakes are alike, and the art of photographing snowflakes is fascinating, but it is not one that younger readers will sit still for.

Snowflake Bentley is also an example of a picture book biography that will provide an introduction to the life of an important person without having to read an entire 100-page biography or encyclopedia article. The picture book biography category is growing with books like *When Marian Sang*, by Pam Munoz Ryan. Of course, older students will need to do further research if they are studying an individual person or time period, but to have the whole class learn about some of the people and accomplishments of an era in a short, engaging format is a wonderful gift.

Marian Anderson was the first black woman to sing with the Metropolitan Opera. *When Marian Sang* tells the story of Anderson's struggle with racism, helping the reader understand the importance of her accomplishment. Students may remember and understand the significance of the event more by reading the picture book than if they simply skimmed a paragraph in a history book.

Picture books are also a great way to give students an introduction or example for writing. Rather than reading a whole novel, a teacher can select a picture book with great characterization, description, voice, word choice, metaphor, or other features to serve as an example before students attempt to write using one of these literary devices. A picture book is less intimidating to the reluctant writer than a full essay or novel and gives the student a sense of confidence that she, too, could produce good voice or use alliteration in her writing. Many of the picture books featured in this book are suitable for use with writing lessons. See Jane Heitman's Linworth book *Teach Writing to Older Readers with Picture Books* for more details on this topic.

Picture books that feature a single poem are good examples of finding meaning in a poem, and a single poem illustrated by two different artists in picture book form can provide a great lesson for comparing and contrasting the artists' views of the poem. Seeing two illustrations of the same text also allows the student to see that two interpretations of the same words can be equally valid. Picture books containing short collections of poetry with illustrations are also helpful in teaching poetry. Books featuring some of the more accessible poems by a specific poet are useful as introductions to famous poets whom students will meet again later in their studies.

In art class, picture books can provide invaluable examples of different techniques, styles, and interpretations, as well as the use of light and texture, and they can show how the illustrator can extend meaning beyond the text. Thomas Locker's book *Sky Tree* features a tree on a knoll in many seasons, weather, and light. The illustrations are ideal for seeing the way one identical scene can change when viewed at different times of the day and seasons of the year. Locker includes poetry as well, so this book can be used for science (the study of seasons), art (light and technique), and language arts (poetry). Picture books with strong art and a weak story (or the opposite) can also be good examples for showing the need for a balance of text and illustration to make a successful book. Again, comparing two or more artists' responses to the same text is possible with stories reissued with new illustrations, or traditional tales illustrated by various artists.

Carefully selected picture books can help students learn the basics of literary criticism and facilitate the development of Literature Circles. By using a picture book for the beginning lessons on a new type of literary criticism, one can teach the elements of discussion, going on to more difficult essays or novels when the process has been practiced using the shorter text. Literature Circles are tools in the teaching of reading in many classrooms, and involve a small group reading the same story, much like a book club, but in a more formal way. Many teachers assign each member of the group a role (facilitator, word finder, note taker, etc.) to help the group run smoothly. When learning to manage literature circles in reading workshop, students need to practice the various roles and learn how to make the discussions work well independent of the teacher. A picture book is an easy tool for practicing these roles before going on to a meatier novel. While *Speak to their Hearts* does not include an entire chapter on literature circles or literary criticism, many of the titles included in this book will be valuable for these purposes.

Picture books can be a useful tool for teachers of grades four through twelve, and a carefully selected library of picture books is invaluable. In the chapters that follow, many examples of exemplary picture books are provided for the librarian and teacher who wish to try this wonderful, flexible format.

Chapter 2

Humor in Picture Books

rior knowledge, context, and developmental level are keys to understanding humor. Many humorous picture books will work with multiple ages, up to and including adults. The key is to match the book to the class or audience. Objectives for using a funny book will range from sheer pleasure or entertainment to the study of puns, idioms, satire, parody, and much more.

Prior knowledge is critical in many ways. It may be as simple as knowing the traditional versions of nursery rhymes and fairy tales or as complex as familiarity with parodies, satires, and more sophisticated forms of word play. The book *Tough Cookie*, by David Wisniewski, requires knowledge of the old, mostly black and white movies and television shows featuring the hard-boiled detective, as it is a take-off on those movies, set inside the cookie jar, with "Fingers" as the bad guy. Margi Palatini's *The Web Files* spoofs the old *Dragnet* television series, complete with the "Dum de dum dum" music.

Sometimes, the librarian or teacher must provide common prior knowledge before reading a book to students. Showing a bit of the *Dragnet* series to students before reading *The Web Files* will be helpful in setting the stage for understanding the humor. For most adults, this step will not be necessary, as many adults remember the Jack Webb version of *Dragnet* from reruns if not from their childhood.

Context is important in all writing. We have all seen examples of the harm done when someone's comment is taken out of context, changing the intended meaning. Meaning and context are important elements of humor. Humor is often based on misunderstandings, misapplication, or mistaken emphasis. Puns and word play fit in this category. Consider the classic Amelia Bedelia books. When Amelia's boss asks her to "pick up the house," she interprets the request literally. Hilarity ensues as she tries to lift the house into the air.

Developmental level is the third important factor in choosing humorous books to use with students. For instance, the only people on the planet who go into gales of laughter with the "Why did the chicken cross the road?" joke are second graders. In the book *Why the Chicken Crossed the Road*, David McCauley translates the old joke into story form, providing readers with a delightful circular story that, like the chicken, has no real answer for how and why the whole thing started. Puns are more subtle and require a developmental level that allows for a more complete understanding of multiple meanings of words, homophones, and words close in sound. Some texts require a level of maturity because of their content, such as Jon Scieszka's *Squids Will Be Squids*, a book of modern day fables. Familiarity with fables is useful for this book, as well as knowledge of the day-to-day trials and tribulations of middle and high school students. For example, one fable is about remembering to call home if you are going to be late—an experience all teenagers can relate to, but not a part of a younger child's life.

 ## Fractured Fairy Tales

This genre has been very popular in the past few years, and many fine examples are available. To appreciate the parody, the student must have a good grounding in the traditional versions of the fairy tales. For many children, the Disney movies may be their only experience with the tales. While Disney did a wonderful job on some fairy tales, now classics themselves, they are sometimes quite different from the Grimms's originals. Activities provided here can be used with any of the fractured fairy tales. The bibliography includes book-specific activities where they apply.

One of the best and most fun writing activities is to create a fractured fairy tale of your own after studying many versions of one particular fairy tale, including both traditional and fractured versions. One strategy is to brainstorm some of the formulas in fairy tales, such as the following: Events happen in threes. The number seven is important. Magical events and characters are involved. Characters can include kings, queens and other royalty, dragons, knights, talking animals, fairies, witches, and magical creatures. When writing a fractured fairy tale, it is best to start with one change to the tale. For instance, changing the three pigs to three wolves begins to generate ideas about the identity of their enemy, how innocent wolves would behave, and so on.

Another current trend in fractured fairy tales is combining the fairy tales. The Three Pigs may make an appearance in Red Riding Hood's neighborhood, or the Big Bad Wolf may find himself visiting the Three Bears. Reading some of these mixtures will also give students ideas about their own versions of the tales. Have students combine two fairy tales into one fractured fairy tale. Imagining how the characters would relate will spark some creativity.

The fairy tale variants here are organized by tale, followed by stories featuring characters from more than one story.

The Three Pigs

Scieszka, Jon, *The True Story of the Three Pigs by A. Wolf; as told to Jon Scieszka.* Illus. Lane Smith. New York: Viking, 1989. (Grades 4-12)

Summary: This is the story of the Three Pigs told from the perspective of the wolf. Alexander T. Wolf claims he is innocent—he was framed! He tells his story from his jail cell, a wrongfully convicted felon. All he wanted to do was borrow a cup of sugar to make a birthday cake for his granny. The huffing and puffing was due to a cold. This is a hilarious spoof on the Three Pigs.

Discussion Questions:

- Which parts of the wolf's claims are believable, which are not?

- What are the clues in the wolf's story that give away his guilt?

- If you were the wolf and wanted to prove your innocence, what would you tell the police?

Activities:

- Have students pretend they are the prosecutor or the defense lawyer in T. Wolf's case. Each lawyer must prepare a case and write a legal brief for the judge. This activity can be a writing assignment or a full mock trial with a jury, judge, witnesses, and victims as well as the lawyers.

- Have students write a persuasive essay telling why Alexander T. Wolf is innocent or guilty. Some may choose to write the essay from the perspective of the pigs.

Book Links: Jon Scieszka

Scieszka, Jon, and Lane Smith. *The Stinky Cheese Man and Other Fairly Stupid Tales.* Illus. Daniel Adel. New York: Viking, 1992. (Grades 4-8)

Summary: These "fairly stupid" stories are very short parodies of many different fairy tales. They are sarcastic fun and may be familiar to many students. They include the Really Ugly Duckling, The Tortoise and the Hair, Cinderumplestiltskin, Little Red Running Shorts, Jack's Bean Problem, and others.

Scieszka, Jon. *The Book That Jack Wrote.* Illus. Daniel Adel. New York: Viking, 1994. (Grades 4-12)

Summary: This cumulative tale based on *The House that Jack Built* begins with a blind rat falling into the book that Jack wrote. As the chain of events continues, the characters are done in, one by one, until only the book remains. Scieszka uses his most twisted humor here, making the tale a fun introduction to parody.

Book Links: The Three Pigs

Wiesner, David. *The Three Pigs.* New York: Clarion Books, 2001. (Grades 4-7)

Summary: In this Caldecott Award winner, Wiesner has taken the pigs literally out of the pages of the story. One of the charms of this book is that when the pigs go outside the storybook pages, they are true-to-life identifiable breeds of pigs. The blend of different art styles in the same pictures is unique and worth studying in art class. In their attempt to escape the wolf, the three pigs meet the cow who jumped over the moon, the cat and the fiddle, and a dragon.

Lowell, Susan. *The Three Little Javelinas*. Illus. Jim Harris. Flagstaff, AZ: Northland Publishing, 1992. (Grades 4-7)

Summary: This is a Southwestern version of the Three Pigs, set in the Sonoran Desert. The pigs are wild peccaries, or javelinas, a very hairy wild pig. A coyote, the sneaky trickster of Native American lore, plays the character of the wolf. These pigs build their houses out of tumbleweeds, saguaro cactus ribs, and adobe bricks. Inside the brick house is a wood stove with a stovepipe for a chimney, leading the coyote to a sizzling end.

Kellogg, Steven. *The Three Little Pigs*. New York: Morrow, 1997. (Grades 4-7)

Summary: In Kellogg's version Serifina Sow, the mother of the Three Pigs, is an entrepreneur who starts a waffle business to support her young family. The Three Pigs inherit the business when Serifina retires to the Gulf of Pasta. When Tempesto the Wolf comes along, things get predictably difficult for the Three Pigs. Mom comes out of retirement to save the day, putting the waffle iron in the fireplace just in time to bake, butter, and syrup Tempesto into submission. The waffle business thrives thereafter, and the Three Pigs marry and make Serifina a busy grandmother, while Tempesto retires to the Gulf of Pasta.

McNaughton, Colin. *Yum!* San Diego: Harcourt Brace, 1999. (Grades 4-7)
McNaughton, Colin. *Preston's Goal.* San Diego: Harcourt Brace, 1998. (Grades 4-7)
McNaughton, Colin. *Oops!* San Diego: Harcourt Brace, 1997. (Grades 4-7)
McNaughton, Colin. *Suddenly!* San Diego: Harcourt Brace, 1995. (Grades 4-7)

Summary: Preston Pig is a fumble-fingered little pig who constantly outwits the Big Bad Wolf through sheer good luck. The sarcastic tone of the wolf's banter is great fun, especially when he seems to talk directly to the reader. Preston is popular with younger kids, as is evidenced by the publication of lift-the-flap and board books featuring the little pig, but the broad humor here is fun for older students in upper elementary grades.

Book Links: Goldilocks and the Three Bears

Stanley, Diane. *Goldie and the Three Bears*. New York: HarperCollins, 2003. (Grades 4-12)

Summary: Goldie knows precisely what she likes and dislikes. When she likes something, she loves it with all her heart. What she has not found is a true best friend. Then one day, she gets off the bus at the wrong stop and enters a house looking for a phone. Of course, the family is not home, and Goldie helps herself. When the three bears return, they find Goldie in Baby Bear's bed. Baby Bear, a little girl bear, is delighted and the two become "just right" friends.

MacDonald, Alan. *Beware of the Bears!* Illus. Gwyneth Williamson. Waukesha, WI: Little Tiger Press, 1998. (Grades 4-7)

Summary: This book will serve as a good example for writing sequels to fairy tales. The Three Bears decide to have their revenge on Goldilocks, so they send Baby Bear to tail Goldilocks and find out where she lives. They go to the house and have a grand time trashing it, having food fights in the kitchen, jumping on the furniture, having a splashing good time in the bathroom and generally wrecking things. When Goldilocks returns, she has a surprise for them—this is not her house, just another she had visited without permission. Imagine the consternation when Goldilocks and the Three Bears find out that the house belongs to none other than the Big Bad Wolf!

Tolhurst, Marilyn. *Somebody and the Three Blairs*. Illus. Simone Abel. New York: Orchard Books, 1991. (Grades 4-7)

Summary: While this book is widely loved by younger children, it is an excellent example of changing one thing and making the whole story different as the change works through the writing. In this case, the change is that "Somebody" is a young bear who comes upon a house, and the Blairs are a family of people who have gone out for a walk. "Somebody" experiments with some of the modern conveniences, opening the freezer, using the shower and finding the rain too hot, and generally making a mess. When the Blairs return from their walk to discover the havoc wreaked by "Somebody", Baby Blair's comments always cut right to the chase; he says "Naughty!" when he sees the kitchen mess, and "Issa big teddy bear" as he discovers the bear in bed.

Book Links: Rapunzel

Roberts, Lynn. *Rapunzel: A Groovy Fairy Tale*. Illus. David Roberts. New York: Harry Abrams, 2003. (Grades 4-12)

Summary: In this 1970s version of the fairy tale, Aunt Esme has Rapunzel locked up in her high-rise apartment. Rapunzel's long red braid is Esme's transportation to and from the apartment. Aunt Esme is an evil school lunch lady who rides a motorcycle. Rapunzel listens to disco and David Bowie, but has no contact with the outside world. Her prince is Roger, a teenage boy who has a rock band. Aunt Esme discovers Roger and casts Rapunzel out on the street, leaving Roger with her long red braid and a case of amnesia. Of course, they find each other, and Rapunzel joins Roger's band.

Book Links: Cinderella

Jackson, Ellen. *Cinder Edna*. Illus. Kevin O'Malley. New York: Lothrop, Lee and Shepard, 1994. (Grades 4-12)

Summary: Cinder Edna and Cinderella live next door to one another. While each has wicked, demanding stepmothers and stepsisters, they are very different. Beautiful Cinderella sits in the ashes wallowing in self-pity. Edna is not beautiful but is quite resourceful. She cleans birdcages for pocket money, knows sixteen different recipes for tuna casserole, and can tell a good joke. Cinderella's fairy godmother outfits her and sends her to the ball where she meets her handsome prince. Cinder Edna does not believe in fairy godmothers, but has a gown on layaway for just such an occasion. Edna takes the bus to the palace, where she meets Rupert, the Prince's younger brother. Rupert is far from handsome, but loves tuna casserole and runs the recycling plant out behind the castle. Both girls get their prince, but only one lives happily ever after.

Book Links: *The Little Red Hen*

Sturges, Philemon. *The Little Red Hen (makes a pizza)*. Illus. Amy Walrod. New York: Dutton, 1999. (Grades 4-7)

Summary: In this urban version of The Little Red Hen, Hen decides to make a pizza. Each time she discovers she is missing a utensil (pizza pan) or an ingredient, she asks who will go to the store. Dog, Cat, and Duck are too busy playing in the street to help. Red Hen goes to the hardware store, the grocery store, and the deli by herself, always buying what she needs—and some other stuff. Her pizza turns out huge, and she invites Dog, Cat, and Duck to share. In the end, her friends volunteer to do the dishes.

Book Links: *Jack and the Beanstalk*

Osborne, Mary Pope. *Kate and the Beanstalk*. Illus. Giselle Potter. New York: Atheneum, 2000. (Grades 4-12)

Summary: This feminist version of the Jack and the Beanstalk story features Kate, who is quite a plucky heroine. She climbs the beanstalk and beats the giant and his wife three times, each time disguised differently. In the end, she discovers that the castle in the clouds was her home before the giant killed her father. Having proven her worth by beating the giant, she inherits the castle and lives happily ever after.

Book Links: *Chicken Little*

Kellogg, Steven. *Chicken Little*. New York: Mulberry Books, 1985. (Grades 4-12)

Summary: Foxy Loxy, a suspect in some poultry kidnappings, is watching when an acorn hits Chicken Little on her way to school. When she cries that the sky is falling and other barnyard birds gather around her, Foxy begins to plan his poultry menus for the near future. He disguises himself as a police officer, and tricks the gathered birds into a paddy wagon. As Foxy taunts Chicken Little, he throws the acorn into the sky, where it causes the real police helicopter to crash, flattening the fleeing fox.

Palatini, Margie. *Earthquack!* Illus. Barry Moser. New York: Simon and Schuster, 2002. (Grades 4-7)

Summary: As Chucky Ducky comes back to the barnyard after swimming his morning laps, the earth rumbles under his feet. He is convinced that it is an earthquake. In the tradition of Chicken Little, he rushes to tell all the other animals of the quake. Part of the fun of this book is the lively language, for instance,

Chucky's repeated insistence, "I heard what I heard. I felt what I felt. I saw what I saw—and I saw it!" When a hungry weasel decides to take advantage of the panicked farm animals and herds them all into his den for his dinner, the plot thickens. The rumbling of the earth reveals the weasel's disguise just in time to save the day. In the end, the earthquake turns out to be two mole brothers, Joel and Lowell, tunneling through on their way to San Jose.

Blended Fractured Fairy Tales

Ada, Alma Flor. *Dear Peter Rabbit*. Illus. Leslie Tryon. New York: Atheneum, 1994. (Grades 4-12)

Ada, Alma Flor. *Yours Truly, Goldilocks*. Illus. Leslie Tryon. New York: Atheneum, 1998. (Grades 4-12)

Ada, Alma Flor. *With Love, Little Red Hen*. Illus. Leslie Tryon. New York: Atheneum, 2001. (Grades 4-12)

Summary: These three titles are excellent examples of fractured fairy tales that mix up the characters from different tales. They are also useful for teaching letter writing. In all three stories, the residents of the "Hidden Forest" write friendly letters to one another. There is no narrative text, only the letters, which require the reader to read between the lines, so to speak, to figure out the story. The characters include Red Riding Hood, Turkey Lurkey, Wolfy Lupus and Fer O'cious, (both bad wolves), three pigs, Goldilocks and her Grandmother, Peter Rabbit and his family and many others. Most of the characters are from the traditional fairy tales, but the author has added some spice with the wolves and a few other original characters.

Activities:

- Individual students can write a story completely in letters to and from the characters. This might be quite challenging, so plan accordingly. Provide students with a graphic organizer or plot outline to help them plan what the plot will be before attempting the actual letters.

- Break the class into two groups, each representing a character. Work together as a class to plan the setting for the story, and then have one group write a letter to the other group. When the second group receives the letter, have them compose a reply. This works in much the same way as the old game where you go around a group and each person adds a sentence to a story. The first letter will need to be sure to pose a problem for one of the characters. The response will need to make the story move along with advice, action taken, or a complication.

Book Links: More Blended Tales

Fearnley, Jan. *Mr. Wolf and the Three Bears*. New York: Harcourt, 2001. (Grades 4-8)

Summary: It is Baby Bear's birthday, and Mr. Wolf is having a birthday party for him. Grandma Wolf comes to help with the preparations, and they cook up a storm, making something special for each of the three bears. The two wolves consult cookbooks, a magazine, a cooking show on television, and the Internet to find the perfect recipes. When all is ready, the three bears arrive, accompanied by the worst party guest ever—Goldilocks! This Goldilocks is particularly wicked, but Grandma Wolf saves the day by making sure that she comes to a fitting end. End papers feature recipes from the story. The Web site the wolves visit is really the author's Web site, <www.hungry-wolf.com>, where you can find all the recipes used in the book along with Grandma Wolf's kitchen tips.

Wiesner, David. *The Three Pigs*. New York: Clarion Books, 2001. See annotation on page 17.

Scieszka, Jon, *The Frog Prince, Continued*. Illus. Steve Johnson. New York: Viking, 1992. (Grades 4-12)

Summary: The princess kisses the frog, he becomes a prince, and they live happily ever after. That is what his book says, but the frog prince finds that both he and the princess are unhappy. He runs off into the forest to find a witch to turn him back into a frog. He visits Sleeping Beauty's witch, Snow White's witch, and Hansel and Gretel's witch and finally meets Cinderella's Fairy Godmother, who turns him into a frog carriage and leaves him alone in the forest. There he has time to think and repent his hasty decision. When midnight strikes and he turns back into a prince, he goes home and kisses his wife. They both turn into frogs and hop off happily ever after.

Palatini, Margie. *Bad Boys*. Illus. Henry Cole. New York: HarperCollins, 2003. (Grades 4-8)

Summary: Palatini mixes up the fairy tales with this story of two wolf brothers who fancy themselves very bad. They are on the run from Red Riding Hood and the Three Pigs, and out of breath, so they decide to hide among a flock of sheep. They dress themselves up and enter the flock, claiming to be two of the "Peep Sheep" who wandered away from Little Bo Peep. They do not fool Betty Mutton, one of the smarter sheep. Betty tricks the boys into getting in line for shearing, which exposes their ruse to the rest of the flock. The many sheep puns make this book good for a writing lesson.

 Nursery Rhyme Parodies

Palatini, Margie. *The Web Files*. Illus. Richard Egielski. New York: Hyperion, 2001. (Grades 4-12)

Summary: Ducktective Web and his partner Bill are hot on the trail of someone who "pilfered a peck of perfect purple almost pickled peppers." As they round up the "usual suspects," (Jack Horner and Little Boy Blue), more vegetables are vanishing. This book echoes the old *Dragnet* television series, complete with the music and the statements of time and place. (11:43 AM, The Squad Room.) Of course, Ducktective Web "quacks" the case and arrests "That Dirty Rat."

Activities:

- To set up prior knowledge for appreciation of the parody, play a few minutes of the old detective series *Dragnet*. Showing the opening sequence and a few minutes of the program should be enough to set up the story. Read the book aloud after showing the video clip.

- Palatini makes frequent use of alliteration. Have students find and list examples from the text. Students can create their own alliterative phrases and sentences.

- As Ducktective Web and Bill go through the police station, they see Miss Muffett, who has been "tossed out of her tuffet," Peep who lost her sheep, three tailless blind mice and others. Any of these characters could provide inspiration for a crime for Ducktective Web and Bill to solve, or students could invent a new criminal at the farm and write another episode of *The Web Files*.

Palatini, Margie. *Piggie Pie*. Illus. Howard Fine. New York: Clarion Books, 1995. (Grades 4-12)

Summary: Gritch the Witch longs to make a piggie pie, so she flies to Old McDonald's Farm (she found it in the yellow pages—call EIEIO) to get some porkers. The piggies find out she is coming and disguise themselves as other animals and even Old McDonald himself. In the end, Gritch meets the wolf, and the two go off together for lunch, each imagining the other as the main course! Have students write a sequel to *Piggie Pie*, then share Palatini's sequel, *Zoom Broom*. Gritch appears again in *Broom Mates*, when her sister comes to visit. Palatini's website, <www.margiepalatini.com>, includes study guides, bookmarks, activities, and games to go with her books.

Book Links: Margie Palatini

Palatini, Margie. *Zoom Broom*. Illus. Howard Fine. New York: Hyperion, 1998. (Grades 4-12)

Palatini, Margie. *Broom Mates*. Illus. Howard Fine. New York: Hyperion, 2003. (Grades 4-12)

Palatini, Margie. *The Perfect Pet*. Illus. Bruce Whatley. New York: HarperCollins, 2003. (Grades 4-7)

Palatini, Margie. *Moosetache*. Illus. Henry Cole. New York: Hyperion, 1997. (Grades 4-8)

Palatini, Margie. *Mooseletoe*. Illus. Henry Cole. New York: Hyperion, 2000. (Grades 4-8)

Palatini, Margie. *Moosekitos: A Moose Family Reunion*. Illus. Henry Cole. New York: Hyperion, 2004. (Grades 4-8)

Other Humorous Picture Books

Scieszka, Jon, and Lane Smith. *Math Curse*. New York: Viking, 1995. (Grades 4-12)

Summary: Ms. Fibonacci tells her students that everything in life can be seen as a math problem, thereby putting a "Math Curse" on the main character, a girl. She begins seeing math problems in everyday events and situations, with hilarious results. Even the dedications in this book are math problems! The "about the author" page is a Venn diagram listing Scieszka's and Lane's books. Scieszka practically invites sequels when Ms. Fibonacci begins the next school day by telling students that everything in life can be seen as a science problem.

Discussion Questions:

- The teacher's name is Fibonicci. What is the significance of that?

- Some questions in this book have no answers, such as "When will Uncle Zeno quit sending me such ugly shirts?" Can you find other unanswerable questions?

- In the math problems given, some of the information is there for the humor value and would not be helpful in solving the problem. Sometimes, story problems do contain irrelevant information. How do you determine what is relevant to solving the problem?

- What will the next day be like if there is a Science Curse?

Activities:

- Do the math! *Math Curse* includes scores of problems of varying difficulty. Complete a selection of problems as a class activity, and assign some to small groups to solve and share solutions.

- In small groups, students can design problems that relate to real life, using the problems in this book as examples.

- Give students an answer and have them work out a problem to fit the answer. All groups will come up with different problems.

- Research Fibonacci numbers. What are they and how do they work?

Deedy, Carmen Agra. *The Library Dragon*. Illus. Michael P. White. Atlanta, GA: Peachtree, 1994. (Grades 4-8)

Summary: Librarians often read this book to primary school students, but much of the rich word play and visual humor escapes the younger children. Sunrise Elementary hires a new librarian, Miss Lotta Scales, who is a real dragon. From the newspaper ad asking for a "thick skinned professional" who can "reduce inventory damage and loss" to the razor wire on the tops of the stacks and the singed students and teachers, this book is full of both written and visual puns. Even the principal, Lance Shields, whose tie bears pictures of shields and swords, does not escape the dragon's fire. It takes a nearsighted reader, Molly Brickmeyer, to tame the Library Dragon through the magic of story time. As Lotta Scales reads a story, her scales fall away, and she becomes Miss Lottie, the librarian.

Activities:

- Students can find and list the many examples of word play and visual puns.

- The library rules set by Miss Lottie are great fun but also very practical. Use this book as an introduction to the library, brainstorming rules for library manners with students.

- Use *The Library Dragon* as a model for students in the art of combining text and illustrations to build a more complete story. Many of the jokes are not within the text, but in the pictures. The illustrator has added to the playful spirit of the text with the many visual puns. Students can try to add to a story they have written with illustrations.

Teague, Mark. *Dear Mrs. LaRue: Letters from Obedience School.* New York: Scholastic, 2002. (Grades 4-12)

Summary: Ike is a bad dog. He has behavior issues, so, Mrs. LaRue, his owner, sends him to Brotwieler Canine Academy, an obedience school for dogs. Ike writes letters to Mrs. La Rue complaining about conditions at the school and denying wrongdoing in his past escapades at home. Pictures in color show the truth, while Ike's version is in black and white. Ike portrays the obedience school as a prison, while the reader sees that his description is an almost total exaggeration. Ike escapes and eventually finds his way home just in time to rescue Mrs. LaRue from an oncoming truck, thus, saving the day.

Discussion Questions:

- Ike's view of his behavior differs drastically from Mrs. LaRue's version. Whose view is most accurate? Is there some truth to each version of events?

- Is Ike telling the truth about his experiences at the Brotwieler Canine Academy? What would the teachers at the academy say about Ike? Would they agree with the content of his letters?

Activities:

- Use this book to serve as an example for letter writing and point of view. Have students imagine they are one of the other dogs at the Academy and write home about Ike, the new student in the school.

- Students can write about the same event from the point of view of different characters. Choose a short excerpt from a news story or show a scene from a movie and have students write from the perspective of one of the characters.

- Select an event that happened in school, at an assembly, on the playground or in the classroom, and have students write what they saw and heard. Compare different students' versions of the event.

Nolen, Jerdine. *Plantzilla.* Illus. David Catrow. New York: Harcourt, 2002. (Grades 4-12)

Summary: Mortimer Henryson writes to his teacher, Mr. Lester, asking to take care of one of the plants for the summer. He gets Plantzilla, the plant he liked best at school. As the summer passes, Plantzilla grows and changes becoming more human;

eating meat and helping around the house. It becomes a bit creepy when Plantzilla seems to have eaten the dog, but things eventually work out. The story is told entirely in letters between Mortimer and his parents and Mr. Lester, the teacher on vacation. David Catrow's pictures tell more than half the story, making the book a strong, funny meld of pictures and words.

Wisniewski, David. *The Secret Knowledge of Grownups*. New York: Lothrop, Lee and Shepard, 1998. (Grades 4-12)

Wisniewski, David. *The Secret Knowledge of Grownups: The Second File*. New York: Lothrop, Lee and Shepard, 2001. (Grades 4-12)

Summary: The premise of these two titles is that all adults participate in a conspiracy to suppress the real, sinister reasons for everyday rules. David Wisniewski claims to have gone undercover to discover the true reasons behind all of these grownup rules. For each of the rules, he includes a log of his undercover activity, the official reason for the rule, and THE TRUTH. The true reasons are the bulk of the text, revealing complex, absurd, but hysterically funny reasons for adult rules. For instance, "Grownup Rule #37, Drink Plenty of Milk." Official Reason, "It's good for you." The Truth is "to keep our atomic cows from exploding." Thus begins four pages of details about the 1960s race with the Russians to develop the first atomic cow and the dire consequences of atomic cow explosions. From combing your hair to not eating too much junk food, Wisniewski's rules and reasons make for a wonderfully funny read aloud.

Activities:

- After reading several selections, choose one rule and have students predict the secret reasons for the rule. Compare student-generated ideas with Wisniewski's version of the "truth."

- Have students "research" a grownup rule Wisniewski did not cover and write the real reason behind the rule.

- In some cases, as in the atomic cows, Wisniewski is spoofing real historical events. High school students can find the parallels between the text and history.

Scieszka, Jon, and Lane Smith. *Squids Will Be Squids: Fresh Morals, Beastly Fables*. New York: Viking, 1998. (Grades 4-12)

Summary: The subjects of these wacky fables are the stuff of teenage life: curfews, homework, television commercials, and arguments. Each tale is short and ends, of course, with a moral. Use this book along with traditional fables as a model for writing modern fables.

Wisniewski, David. *Tough Cookie*. New York: Lothrop, Lee and Shepard, 1999. (Grades 4-12)

Summary: This is a take-off on the old detective movies from the Humphrey Bogart era. The hard-boiled detective in this case is a cookie—and he lives in the world of the Cookie Jar. The story begins with a poster from the Jar Transit Authority, welcoming new cookies to the Jar. Freshness decides your level in the cookie society. Predictably, the bottom of the jar is the rough neighborhood where the crumbs live. The main character, Tough Cookie, has fallen on hard times. When Tough Cookie discovers that the notorious criminal, "Fingers," has grabbed and bitten his old partner, "Chips," he and his crumb friends must rise to the rescue.

Cronin, Doreen. *Click, Clack, Moo: Cows that Type*. Illus. Betsy Lewin. Simon and Schuster: 2000. (Grades 4-12)

Cronin, Doreen. *Giggle, Giggle, Quack*. Illus. Betsy Lewin. Simon and Schuster: 2002. (Grades 4-12)

Cronin, Doreen. *Duck for President*. Illus. Betsy Lewin. Simon and Schuster: 2004. (Grades 4-12)

Summary: This series is full of mature themes and jokes. Use them as fun read alouds, or consider using *Click Clack Moo* when learning about strikes and *Duck for President* near election time.

In *Click, Clack, Moo*, the cows find a typewriter and begin leaving Farmer Brown messages. The cows and chickens go on strike—no milk, no eggs—until Farmer Brown meets their demands for electric blankets. Farmer Brown is livid, but the strikers hold firm. Duck, as a neutral party, helps negotiate a compromise.

Duck become the focus of the story in *Giggle, Giggle, Quack*. Farmer Brown goes on vacation, leaving his brother Bob in charge. Farmer Brown leaves written instructions for Bob, but Duck finds a pencil and replaces the farmer's notes with his own versions. Consequently, the animals have pizza for dinner, Bob treats the pigs to bubble baths, and the cows choose the movie for movie night *(The Sound of Moosic)*. All is well until Farmer Brown calls during movie night!

In *Duck for President*, Duck decides his chores are too hard and stages an election for leadership of the farm. The animals register to vote, and Duck beats Farmer Brown by a narrow margin. Managing the farm is harder than he thought, so, Duck goes on to run successfully for Governor, and then, President. This book is full of modern day election humor. Duck's campaign tactics include kissing babies, giving "speeches only other ducks could understand," and playing the saxophone on late night television. His campaign slogans are hilariously familiar. When the job of President proves too hard, Duck retires to the farm to write his autobiography. Look for the famous first lines on his computer screen.

Donnelly, Jennifer. *Humble Pie*. Illus. Stephen Gammell. New York: Atheneum, 2002. (Grades 4-8)

Summary: Theo is an obnoxious, greedy, rude, self-centered kid. His parents spoil him rotten. To teach Theo a lesson, Grandmother makes a huge Humble Pie. When Theo reaches for a taste of the pie filling, he falls in. Grandmother seals him up in the pie. The pie will roll on edge, so, Theo rolls about, trying to get someone to help him get out. The neighbors will not help, as they are all quite sick of his behavior. His family seems very happy without him as well, which gives him "food" for thought. He rolls into a very poor village nearby, and upon seeing the villagers plight, begins to feel empathy for the first time. Just as the starving villagers prepare to bake the wonderful pie, Theo pops out and runs back home, humbled and much better behaved. The magical pie feeds the villagers until their crops come in the next year.

Discussion Questions:

- Was Theo's grandma a witch? The story does not say she is a witch, but the illustrator chose to picture her as one. Would you have chosen to make her look like a witch? Why do you think the illustrator made that choice?

- Did Grandma intend for the pie to end up in the poor village or was that a happy accident? How does it add to the story? Would it have been as good a story without that part?

- How did the pie help the villagers?

- Will Theo's change of personality last? Will he return to his old, spoiled behavior?

Activities:

- The author describes Theo as *obnoxious, obstreperous, high-handed, mouthy, demanding, arrogant, selfish, inconsiderate, thoughtless, and grabby*. Using the dictionary and thesaurus, have students look up the words and compare the meanings. Are they synonyms? Do they describe different behaviors? What do they have in common? Are there other descriptive words that would also fit Theo's behavior at the beginning of the book? Go to the visual thesaurus: <http://www.visualthesaurus.com/online/index.html>, for an animated, graphic representation of related words and their meanings.

- As a follow up to the previous activity, have students generate a list of words that describe Theo after his humbling experience.

- Theo's grandmother said he got his "just desserts." Explore idioms with your students. What did she mean by that saying? Introduce other idioms and discuss their meanings. The book link below lists some other books about idioms. Students can make their own book of idioms and their definitions.

Book Links: Idioms

Gwynne, Fred. *The Sixteen-Hand Horse*. New York: Prentice-Hall, 1980. (Grades 4-8)

Gwynne, Fred. *A Chocolate Moose for Dinner*. New York: Prentice-Hall, 1996. (Grades 4-8)

Leedy, Loreen, and Pat Street. *I Have a Frog in My Throat: 440 Animal Sayings a Little Bird Told Me*. New York: Holiday House, 2003. (Grades 4-12)

Terban, Marvin. *In a Pickle and Other Funny Idioms*. Illus. Giulio Maestro. New York: Clarion Books, 1983. (Grades 4-12)

Terban, Marvin. *The Scholastic Dictionary of Idioms*. New York: Scholastic, 1996. (Grades 4-12)

Terban, Marvin. *Punching the Clock: Funny Action Idioms*. Illus. Tom Huffman. New York: Clarion Books, 1990. (Grades 4-12)

Chapter 3

Science: Using

Picture Books to Illustrate

Science Concepts

Science is by nature a hands-on subject. Observation is one of the most important skills we teach. Students need to learn the scientific method, which includes proposing and testing a hypothesis, observing the results, and synthesizing the information to create a new question. Current science education reforms suggest that inquiry is one of the best ways to teach science. Inquiry science theory tells us that students must experience science as problem solving and begin to think of themselves as scientific and technological problem solvers. While firsthand exploration and investigation are essential in science education, science literature, including picture books, also plays an important part. Prior knowledge helps students form ideas to test, and picture books are a great way to provide some of that prior knowledge in a group setting. Picture books can create a desire to learn more about a science topic. Science is not without controversy and competing theories. Picture books can help raise interest in finding out about different theories and stimulate debates between students about competing theories.

While there are many fine science writers, several authors are worthy of special mention in this chapter. Seymour Simon is perhaps the king of science nonfiction for children. He has written over 150 science books for children, many honored as Outstanding Science Trade Books for Children by the National Science Teachers' Association. He has won numerous other awards for his books. His hallmark is extremely clear, but not overly simplified writing, and stunning photography. He has several series of books on the planets, the human body, and animals. Some of his titles are included in this chapter, where appropriate, however, except for his early reader books, all of his work is eminently suitable for use with older readers. Jim Arnosky is another prolific science writer. He illustrates his books, spending time in the wild to observe his subjects first-hand. His work ranges from very simple books for younger children to books that delight older readers and adults. Jonathan London and Meredith Hooper both use lyrical language to tell science related stories.

Books selected for this chapter range from 32 to 48 pages in length. While some may stretch the definition of picture books because they are longer and tend to tell stories or examine topics that are a bit more complex, they stay within the picture book format. In many cases, discussion questions will arise naturally from or are included in the text, and are not included in the annotations. The annotations in this chapter are arranged by topic.

 # The Elements

Robbins, Ken. *Fire.* New York: Henry Holt, 1996. (Grades 4-12)

Robbins, Ken. *Earth.* New York: Henry Holt, 1995. (Grades 4-12)

Robbins, Ken. *Air.* New York: Henry Holt, 1995. (Grades 4-12)

Robbins, Ken. *Water.* New York: Henry Holt, 1994. (Grades 4-12)

Summary: These four books, together, make up Ken Robbins's series called *The Elements.* Robbins takes photographs in black and white and hand colors them carefully, screening off the parts he does not want affected. This technique lends a drama to his pictures that adds to the overall quality and effect of the books. In each of the books, the text reads as a narrative, continuing from page to page, but each two-page spread features a particular concept, such as, earthquakes, lightning, or making a fire. These books are useful alone as you study the different topics or all together as part of a larger unit on the elements themselves. Discussion questions will flow naturally as you read these books, so no specific questions are listed here.

Activities:

- Research topics appear on virtually every two-page spread in these books as Robbins gives an overview of the subject without going into too much depth. For instance, he lists a few of the thousands of uses humankind has for fire. A group of students could research additional uses for fire, presenting the expanded list as a PowerPoint presentation or a poster. Another group might research the dangers of fire and its misuse for a similar presentation.

- At least once in each book, Robbins makes statements that would lend themselves to debate. For instance, in *Fire*, in the section about firearms, he says, "The truth is—and it's sad to say—most guns are meant to kill people today." What a hot topic for debate! In *Earth*, he mentions that there are too many people on the earth, and we are "in danger of poisoning the earth with our wastes." This is another subject perfect for choosing opposing views. Each side can research its argument and defend its conclusions. Students could prepare for a debate on one of these provocative questions, write a persuasive essay, or prepare an oral presentation or poster taking sides on one of these issues.

- Invite a local photographer in to show the students black and white photographs and discuss the merits of color versus black and white photography. Find a photographer or artist who will demonstrate the technique of tinting photographs and arrange for a demonstration.

Hooper, Meredith. *The Pebble in My Pocket.* Illus. Chris Coady. New York: Viking, 1996. (Grades 4-8)

Summary: The author uses a pebble to tell the story of the evolution of the earth, beginning with volcanoes erupting 480 million years ago. Earthquakes move the earth, weather acts upon the surface, and pieces break off mountains. Boulders erode and are covered and uncovered by the sea as the earth changes. As the eons pass, dinosaurs tread on a rock and the rock becomes a pebble. The pebble lies beside a river until a girl puts it in her pocket. The timelines on the last two pages are color-coded to make it easier to compare the ages of the earth with the life spans of the animal species featured in the book.

Discussion Questions:

- The author describes an event before explaining what caused the action. For instance, the reader sees the land buckling and folding, and then, learns that this motion is caused by two landmasses colliding. As you read the book aloud, stop and ask students why they think these things are happening before going on to the explanation.

- What do you think the pebble will become next? Is it possible for the pebble to wear away into nothing? Where does the matter go?

Activities:

- The text mentions that small mammals scurry around when the dinosaurs are asleep. Students may want to find out what small mammals lived in the time of dinosaurs and if those mammals became extinct along with the dinosaurs.

- Students can research the current theories about the reasons for the extinction of dinosaurs.

- When the author tells the reader about the pebble not moving much since the last Ice Age, the illustrations reflect this concept by showing the passage of time in three picture bands across the page. The pictures show the same landscape in different centuries. Challenge students to show a scene in different seasons or years. Pair this book with *Sky Tree*, by Thomas Locker, where he draws the same tree in different seasons. For a history unit, students could draw the same town in different eras. An example is provided in *A Street Through Time*, by Anne Millard, annotated in Chapter 4.

- The color-coding of the two timelines suggests another way to present information. How do the two timelines mesh? Students could merge the two timelines in their own version, or present information for another report in a similar two-part timeline.

Book Links: Meredith Hooper

Hooper, Meredith. *The Drop in My Drink: The Story of Water on Our Planet.* Illus. Chris Coady. New York: Viking, 1998. (Grades 4-12)

Summary: Water molecules are everywhere on earth, and a drop from the tap is made up of molecules that have been everywhere on earth, via the water cycle. To illustrate the water cycle, the author follows one drop of water on a journey through earth's history. At the end of the book, the author includes information about recycling and taking care of the water supply as well as an illustrated explanation of the water cycle. Some amazing water facts complete the water cycle page.

Hooper, Meredith. *River Story.* Illus. Bee Willey. Cambridge, MA: Candlewick Press, 2000. (Grades 4-8)

Summary: Beautiful art and lyrical prose trace a river from its source to the sea. The illustrations feature different animals who visit the river as it flows to the ocean. A birds-eye view of the entire river system graces the last page. *River Story* will be useful for study of river ecosystems and the water cycle.

Wick, Walter. *A Drop of Water.* New York: Scholastic, 1997. (Grades 4-12)

Summary: Walter Wick has created the most astonishing photographs of water for this book. He explains and illustrates evaporation, condensation, capillary attraction, and surface tension with simple, clear text accompanying his photography. After demonstrating the properties of water, the author recreates experiments with water. The explanations are simple and direct. The main text concludes with a discussion of the water cycle. An appendix informs the reader in detail how to perform the featured experiments, what weather or humidity conditions are necessary for them to work, and in some cases, how to modify the experiment to learn even more. This book can be used a few pages at a time to learn about each of the properties of water or all at once as an introduction to a water unit.

Discussion Questions:

- This book generates many questions from readers. Have students write their questions on sticky notes, one question per sticky note, and jot down the page in the book where clues to the answer should appear. Gather the questions and group them by page to discuss at a different session. Many of the questions will lead right into experiments students will want to perform.

- Ask students to choose the most interesting picture from *A Drop of Water*. Have students share their favorites and the reasons behind their choices.

Activities:

- All of the experiments in this book use simple, everyday materials. Most can be performed by individual students, small groups, or as demonstrations. Wick documented his results with photographs. These experiments would be good ones for teaching scientific observation and documentation by description as well as attempting to photograph some student experiments.

- Students can search the library for books of water experiments to choose different ways of demonstrating the properties of water, and then, perform those experiments as a project for class.

Book Links: Water

Kerley, Barbara. *A Cool Drink of Water*. Washington, DC: National Geographic, 2002. (Grades 4-12)

Summary: This book begins, "Somewhere, right now, someone is drinking water." The main text is essentially a poem, accompanied by photographs of people and water all over the world. At first glance, it seems beautiful and touching but too simple for use with older students, however, a wealth of information is included after the poem ends. A map shows the locations of the photos and thumbnails with brief captions that tell the story behind each picture. An essay on water conservation authored by the President of the National Geographic Society completes the book. This book will be valuable to use with *A Drop of Water* by Wick or Ken Robbins's *Water*.

Locker, Thomas. *Water Dance*. San Diego, CA: Harcourt, 1997. (Grades 4-12)

Summary: In *Water Dance*, Locker illustrates the water cycle. Poetic text accompanies paintings of storm fronts, mist, rain, lakes, and waterfalls. A more detailed scientific explanation of the water cycle is included at the end of the book, pairing a painting with a paragraph about that part of the water cycle.

 # Evolution

Jenkins, Steve. *Life on Earth: The Story of Evolution*. Boston, MA: Houghton Mifflin, 2002. (Grades 4-12)

Summary: *Life on Earth* explores the origin of life on earth and the theory of evolution. The text is simple, but detailed enough to serve as a basic introduction to the topic. Jenkins's trademark art style, cut paper collage set against plain backgrounds, works effectively to clearly and accurately depict the animals. A timeline at the end of the book condenses the 4.5 billion year history of earth into one 24-hour day, to give the reader a better perspective on that immense span of time. A key to the animals portrayed in the book lists their names and indicates when and where they lived, noting those that are extinct. A bibliography is included.

Discussion Questions:

- Discuss the difference between mutation and variation. How do they work together to produce evolutionary changes in species?

- What questions do you have about evolution after reading this book? Where might you go for more information?

Activities:

- Steve Jenkins has written and illustrated many other science books using cut paper collage. Gather some of his books to do a study of this technique of illustration. Other cut paper artists to include in this study would be Eric Carle, Denise Fleming, Lois Ehlert, and David Wisniewski, among others. Some of these artist create their own paper, some collect handmade paper, and some paint pictures to cut apart and transfer to a background cut from another paper. Students can experiment with different ways of producing cut paper art. See Chapter 6 for a list of books illustrated with collage.

- The idea of equating a long timeline to a single day is intriguing. Challenge students to create a 24-hour timeline depicting the major events of United States history, world history, World War I or II, or any other topics of study.

Book Links: Steve Jenkins

Jenkins, Steve, and Robin Page. *Animals in Flight.* Boston, MA: Houghton Mifflin, 2001. (Grades 4-8)

Summary: There are several levels to this book. The narrative that runs throughout is a quite simple, straightforward text about flight. The main illustration is large and accompanied by a caption. On each two-page spread, the authors have also included small illustrations with more detailed information about each topic. For instance, on a page about wings, there is an illustration showing different kinds of wings and an explanation of how wings provide lift, the force that makes flight possible.

Jenkins, Steve. *Looking Down.* Boston, MA: Houghton Mifflin, 1995. (Grades 4-12)

Summary: This book is notable because it is wordless. It begins by looking at earth and the moon from out in space. The focus gradually narrows, moving toward a child in his backyard. Finally, the reader sees a ladybug under the child's magnifying glass. *Looking Down* is ideal for art classes, discussions of point of view, and understanding maps and aerial photographs. For more examples of narrowing focus, see Istvan Banyai's titles, *Zoom* and *Rezoom*.

Jenkins, Steve. *The Top of the World: Climbing Mount Everest.* Boston, MA: Houghton Mifflin, 1999. (Grades 4-12)

Summary: Jenkins's always-stunning cut paper illustrations work with informative text to tell the sequence of an Everest Climb. Many related facts are contained in sidebars on each page. An endnote shows the relative height of the "Seven Summits," the tallest peaks on each of the continents. A bibliography and a list of Mount Everest records are included. Use this with *The Young Adventurer's Guide to Everest* by Jonathan Chester.

Jenkins, Steve. *Biggest, Strongest, Fastest.* Boston, MA: Houghton Mifflin, 1995. (Grades 4-8)

Jenkins, Steve. *Actual Size.* Boston, MA: Houghton Mifflin, 2004. (Grades 4-8)

Jenkins, Steve. *Hottest, Coldest, Highest, Deepest*. Boston, MA: Houghton Mifflin, 2004. (Grades 4-8)

Jenkins, Steve. *Elephants Swim*. Boston, MA: Houghton Mifflin, 1995. (Grades 4-8)

Jenkins, Steve. *Big and Little*. Boston, MA: Houghton Mifflin, 1996. (Grades 4-8)

Book Links: Evolution

McNulty, Faith. *How Whales Walked into the Sea*. Illus. Ted Rand. New York: Scholastic, 1999. (Grades 4-12)

Summary: This book illustrates for the reader the slow evolution of land animals called Mesorychids into the water mammals we now call whales. The author is careful to point out where science does and does not have full fossil evidence for this progression, but the theory is compelling nonetheless, and the illustrations give an idea of what those different stages of evolution looked like. This book does not go into detail, but will raise curiosity about evolution and natural selection that could spur students to further study.

 # Extinction

Henderson, Douglas. *Asteroid Impact*. New York: Dial, 2000. (Grades 4-12)

Summary: Sixty five million years ago, a large asteroid collided with Earth, theoretically ending the Age of Dinosaurs. *Asteroid Impact* begins with a description of earth during the Cretaceous Period. Before introducing the asteroid into the picture, the author uses a down-to-earth example to illustrate the forces created by such an impact. A car smashes into a house-sized concrete block, first at 60 miles per hour, gradually increasing to the velocity of the asteroid (60,000 MPH), showing the effect of a car/block collision at each speed. The rest of the text shows the sequence of asteroid-related events in the time of dinosaurs. Asteroid questions and answers are included at the end of the book.

Discussion Questions:
Students will generate many questions during a reading of this book. Have students write down their questions as you read the book aloud the first time. Read the book a second time, stopping to discuss student questions.

Activities:

- Research the asteroid impact theory. Do all scientists agree that an asteroid or comet hit the earth, causing the extinction of the dinosaurs? Are there competing theories? What evidence supports each theory?

- Create a science fiction story about a new asteroid approaching the earth in the future. Some students may choose to write the story as if humankind becomes extinct or nearly so, while other students may choose to invent a device that could change the trajectory of the asteroid, thereby saving the earth and its inhabitants from destruction.

Habitats

Hooper, Meredith. *Antarctic Journal.* Illus. Licia deLeiris. Washington, DC: National Geographic Society, 2000. (Grades 4-12)

Summary: The author and illustrator spent one summer at and around Palmer Station on the Antarctic Peninsula. This book is a journal of their experiences. Licia deLeiris uses sketches and watercolor paintings to complement Meredith Hooper's text, which features the various animals that live and breed on the peninsula and the surrounding islands. The book includes a map, an index, and an afterward discussing the Antarctic food chain and the effect of global warming on the animals of Antarctica.

Discussion Questions:

- Everyone at Palmer Station has to sign out when going to the "backyard," as it is safer to know where everyone is at all times. What dangers are on the glacier? Is the glacier as dangerous as going in the boat to an island? Which do you think would be more dangerous?

- When counting penguins, the procedure is to count three times, then average the three totals. Why would it be hard to get an accurate count? Where else might this strategy be useful in daily life? Would it be easier to count nests or penguins?

- What would it feel like to be in a Zodiac, a rubber boat, with a huge humpback whale swimming just underneath you? Would you be frightened? Would you look over the side to see the whale?

Activities:

- Research Palmer Station. How many scientists live there in the summer? Is it a year-round station? What are conditions like on Palmer Station in the winter? What projects are currently in progress at Palmer Station? What other research stations are on the Continent of Antarctica?

- The sketches in this book are a good example for students who are learning to draw. Use them to show students what the artist does to remember what she saw and compare the sketches to the finished paintings in the book.

Book Links: Antarctica

Conlan, Kathy. *Under the Ice.* Toronto, ON, Canada: Kids Can Press, 2002. (Grades 4-12)

Summary: This is a detailed, first person account by a scientist and underwater photographer who spent many summers diving under the ice at McMurdo Station, Antarctica. Her team studied the effects of pollution on the underwater environment. The water ecosystem under the ice is a unique environment, and scientists are learning much about the world's oceans from studies in Antarctica. This book gives information about many topics, including studies of pollution, Antarctica, underwater photography, scuba diving under the ice, and scientific methods. The immediacy of the first person account makes the book especially appealing to readers.

Cerullo, Mary. *Life Under Ice*. Illus. Bill Curtsinger. Gardiner, Maine: Tilbury House, 2003. (Grades 4-12)

Summary: The author tells the story of the photographer who has returned to Antarctica for fifteen summers to take pictures under the ice near McMurdo Station. This book works well paired with *Under the Ice*, focusing more on the animal and plant life and the requirements of diving in such harsh conditions. Together, they make a powerful study of the underwater world of Antarctica.

Book Links: Mary Cerullo

Cerullo, Mary. *Sea Soup: Zooplankton*. Illus. Bill Curtsinger. Gardiner, Maine: Tilbury House, 2001. (Grades 4-12)

Cerullo, Mary. *Sea Soup: Phytoplankton*. Illus. Bill Curtsinger. Gardiner, Maine: Tilbury House, 1999. (Grades 4-12)

Cerullo, Mary. *Sea Turtles: Ocean Nomads*. Illus. Jeffrey Rotman. New York: Dutton, 2003. (Grades 4-12)

Webb, Sophie. *My Season with Penguins: An Antarctic Journal*. Boston, MA: Houghton Mifflin, 2000. (Grades 4-8)

Summary: This is another useful title on Antarctica. The author, a biologist and artist, spent a summer studying Adelie Penguins at Polar Haven, one of several research camps located beside penguin colonies near McMurdo Station. The book is a day-by-day journal of her experience setting up experiments, banding and tracking penguins, and painting the scenes she observed. Webb illustrated the book with watercolor paintings, some done inside the colony while literally surrounded by penguins.

Wright-Frierson, Virginia. *A North American Rain Forest Scrapbook*. New York: Walker, 1999. (Grades 4-12)

Summary: The narrative in this story tells about the author/illustrator's experiences on a visit to the world's largest temperate rain forest, which is located on the Olympic Peninsula in the Olympic National Forest of Washington State. The author drew all of the sketches and pictures. The illustrations resemble photographs, scrapbook and guidebook pages, postcards, and small sketches made in the forest. The narrative carries the story forward, but the treasure in this book is to examine in detail the sketches, the captions for the illustrations, and the beauty of Wright-Frierson's art.

Discussion Questions:

- The author describes taking time to sketch and shoot photographs while in the forest. Can taking pictures and making sketches be a type of research? What did she need to do to find out more information about the things she sketched?

- How much research do you think the author did before going in person to the rain forest? She brought a guidebook along. Could she have studied that before her trip? Would she have made a list of things she wanted to see while she was there?

- Wright-Frierson also includes paintings of herself doing her research. How did she draw those scenes accurately?

Activities:

- This book begs us to go on a walk near our home or school and sketch what we see. Wherever we live, there are wonders of nature, even in the city. Students can observe life on the playground, a nearby nature trail, a city park, a grove of trees, and many other places. A field trip to the zoo or a national, county, or state park could be the culminating activity of a unit on the flora and fauna of a region. Taking sketchbooks and making sketches and notes would be great practice of both art and scientific observation skills.

- Practicing the techniques of sketching without being critical of oneself is difficult for people of all ages. Bring in an art teacher or local artist to teach the rudiments of sketching. Ask the artist to show the students examples from his or her sketchbook. It may surprise students to learn that artists do not complete every picture, but sketch ideas as a way of taking notes, and flesh out some of the pictures later.

- The facts presented in this book do not go into depth, leaving many possible research questions in students' minds. Topics range from simple curiosity about slugs to larger, more essential questions about protection of rain forests. The deliciously gross response to a National Park Ranger licking a slug is motivation enough for some students to research the defense mechanisms of different animals. The near extinction and subsequent revitalization of the Roosevelt Elk population in the Olympic National Forest could be an in-depth investigation for students.

Book Links: Virginia Wright-Frierson

Wright-Frierson, Virginia. *An Island Scrapbook: Dawn to Dusk on a Barrier Island.* New York: Simon & Schuster Books, 1998. (Grades 4-12)

Wright-Frierson, Virginia. *A Desert Scrapbook: Dawn to Dusk in the Sonoran Desert.* New York: Simon & Schuster Books, 1996. (Grades 4-12)

Book Links: Rainforests

Pandell, Karen. *Journey Through the Northern Rainforest.* Photographs by Art Wolfe, Illus. Denise Y. Takahashi. New York: Dutton, 1999. (Grades 4-12)

Summary: This book works on two levels. The first is a straightforward text full of facts about the northern temperate rainforest. The text is a detailed examination of the complexity of life in a rainforest and a discussion of the consequences of razing it. The second level is a look at the forest through the eyes of an eagle. The author introduces a Native American mask carver. His belief is that if someone wears one of his masks, that person will feel the spirit of the animal represented and see through that animal's eyes. A small box on each page tells what the eagle sees.

Lasky, Kathryn. *The Most Beautiful Roof in the World*. Illus. Christopher Knight. New York: Harcourt Brace, 1997. (Grades 4-12)

Summary: This photographic essay details a day in the rainforest. The author tells the story of Meg Lowman, director of research and conservation at The Marie Selby Botanical Gardens, a rainforest research center in Sarasota, Florida. Lowman spends at least five days per month in the canopy of rainforests around the world (in this case in Belize) researching the interactions of insects with plant life. The author and photographer joined her in the canopy to learn about her work. On the day the author documents, Lowman takes her children for their first trip up into the canopy, 150 feet above the forest floor. The author describes the difficulty of ascending to and working in the canopy and the variety of methods for collecting specimens and data in the rainforest.

Batten, Mary. *Aliens From Earth: When Animals and Planets Invade other Ecosystems*. Illus. Beverly J. Doyle. Atlanta, GA: Peachtree, 2003. (Grades 4-12)

Summary: *Aliens From Earth* provides a basic introduction to the problems that nonnative plants and animals cause to native ecosystems. The author tells how and why species move into new habitats and what effect they have on existing populations. The bottom of each page has a list of the animals pictured, with endangered, extinct, native, and alien species in different types of print for easy identification. Students will recognize some of these alien species, such as the domestic cat, fox, rabbit, army ant, and "killer" bee (Africanized honeybee). This book will provide a jumping off point for student research about invasive and alien species and the balance of life in an ecosystem.

Plants

Lucht, Irmgard. *The Red Poppy*. New York: Hyperion, 1994. (Grades 4-12)

Summary: Lyrical text and stunning paintings take the reader through the life cycle of a red poppy. Red poppies bloom for only one day, a very short window for pollination. The artist has created detailed pictures of poppies growing on the edge of wheat fields, the insects and animals that visit the flowers, and the process of pollination. The incredible detail in these paintings comes in part from the use of a binocular microscope or stereoscope, which allows the artist to see tiny things magnified in three dimensions. Endnotes give other facts about the animals featured and about how the artist painted these pictures.

Discussion Questions:

- Look carefully at each picture. How many animals can you find in each picture? You will need to look carefully to see all the animals.

- What does the author mean when she writes, "Color is the language of flowers?" Can you think of plants or animals that send a message with their colors? Do you think that color is a language that people use?

- What will happen if the poppy does not get pollen from another poppy?

Activities:

- This is an ideal book for discovering the names of the parts of a plant or flower. The following words appear in the text: stalk, ear, fruit, bud, stems, sepals, flower, petals, pollen, blossom, pistil, stamens, seed capsule, grains, and seeds. Have students draw and label the parts of a plant.

- Lucht explains her acrylic paint technique in the author's note. Fine arts students may wish to experiment with her method.

- Borrow a stereoscope and assist students in using it to look at small items from nature. Compare the view to that of a standard microscope. Have students try drawing what they see in the stereoscope.

Viera, Linda. *The Ever-Living Tree: The Life and Times of a Coast Redwood.* Illus. Christopher Canyon. New York: Walker, 1994. (Grades 4-12)

Summary: Coast redwood trees can live for over 2,000 years. The featured tree sprouted in the time of Alexander the Great, around 400 BC, and continues to grow today. The narrative provides specific details about the life of the tree, such as surviving a forest fire, coupled with information about the redwood species. To highlight the vast life span of the redwood, the author connects the lifetime of the tree with major events in world history.

 # Migration

Lasky, Kathryn. *Interrupted Journey: Saving Endangered Sea Turtles.* Illus. Christopher Knight. Cambridge, MA: Candlewick, 2001. (Grades 4-8)

Summary: Kemp's Ridley turtles are among the most endangered species in the world. *Interrupted Journey* highlights an international effort to save the turtles. A young turtle becomes lost during migration and ends up on the beaches of Cape Cod. As winter closes in, it becomes too cold for him to survive. A family rescues the turtle and takes him to the New England Aquarium, where a team of workers revives and cares for the young turtle. Eventually, the turtle is strong enough for transfer to Florida, where a wildlife rescue team releases him into his home waters.

Discussion Questions:

- Why do you think no one knows where the turtles go between their hatching and coming back to lay eggs? How would you go about finding out if you were a scientist? What would the difficulties be in such a quest?

- Would you be willing to participate in helping wildlife? Can you think of ways to help the wildlife where you live? Are there things you can do in your everyday life that will make the world safer for wildlife?

Activities:

- Students can research the lives of turtles or another endangered species. Have them begin by writing what they already know, using a KWL Chart (What I KNOW, what I WANT to know, what I LEARNED) to help focus their questions about their chosen animal. Help students develop research questions that lead them to consider the value of the animals and the ways people can protect wildlife rather than the "basic facts" report. For instance, "What do turtles need to survive and thrive?" or "How can I change the behaviors and perceptions people have that contribute to the extinction of turtles?"

- If there is an animal shelter or rescue facility nearby, arrange for a field trip to learn about its work. Help students generate a list of questions for the workers before going on the field trip. Students may wish to follow their trip with raising funds to help the shelter or volunteering to work at the facility.

Davies, Nicola. *One Tiny Turtle*. Illus. Jane Chapman. Cambridge, MA: Candlewick, 2001. (Grades 4-7)

Summary: Beautiful paintings and poetic language tell of the journey of a baby loggerhead turtle from her hatching place on the beach to the sea, then, back years later to the same beach to lay her eggs. This is a simple book, but worthwhile for a second look at the lives of turtles. The text is in two parts: the narrative and extra facts about the turtles. The two kinds of text are in different typeface and artfully placed on the illustrations.

Cherry, Lynne. *Flute's Journey: The Life of a Wood Thrush*. New York: Harcourt Brace, 1997. (Grades 4-7)

Summary: Flute is a wood thrush who migrates from the Belt Woods Preserve in Maryland to the Monteverde Rain Forest in Costa Rica. The part of the forest featured in this story is named Bosque Eterno de los Ninos, or The Eternal Forest of the Children, because children all over the world have raised funds to buy and preserve it. The story follows Flute from his birth in Maryland through his migration and winter in Costa Rica and back to his birthplace. In Maryland, he finds a mate, Feather, and they raise chicks of their own. The author highlights the dangers Flute faces in both forests and along his migration route. Out of two batches of eggs, only two of Flute and Feather's chicks survive, along with the chick of a cowbird, a bird who deposits her egg in the thrush nest. An author's note discusses the dangers faced by migrating birds and gives ideas for helping birds survive.

Discussion Questions:

- In the author's note about the Belt Forest, Cherry tells us that Sexton Belt willed his land to his church with the direction that it stay wilderness forestland. The church went to court and won the right to modify Belt's will and sell the land. Other people fought that decision and were successful. What side of that argument would you choose? Why do you think Mr. Belt wanted the land to remain forested? Why would the church want to sell the forest?

- Do you think Flute and Feather realized the cowbird had tricked them into raising her egg? How did you feel when the cowbird chick took the food that should have fed the third thrush chick?

Activities:

- Research topics suggested by this text include migratory birds, cowbirds, thrush, the Monteverde Forest and the Eternal Forest of the Children, the Belt Woods Preserve, and the actions of the Episcopal Church in regards to Sexton Belt's will. Have students choose a topic of interest and research in the library and on the Internet. The Monteverde Forest is the subject of several Web sites, including <http://academic.evergreen.edu/n/nadkarnn/monteverde/mvhome.html>.

- Students can research the Belt Woods legal case and recreate a court case or stage a debate about the issues involved. This would be a fabulous collaborative project between the librarian and an English or Debate teacher at the high school level.

- Students can write to "Save the Land You Love," as suggested in the author's note, for information about assisting in the survival of songbirds.

- Obtain recordings of bird songs. Practice identifying birds by their songs. Invite a guest speaker to share the techniques of bird identification. Contact local birding groups for resources.

Book Links: Migration

Lerner, Carol. *On the Wing: American Birds in Migration.* NY: HarperCollins, 2001. (Grades 4-8)

Summary: There are several kinds of migration and many variations among migrating birds. The author uses some North American birds as examples as she informs the reader about migration in its many forms. She includes partial migration, migration within the United States and to the southern hemisphere, arctic migrants, and even birds that migrate seasonally from the bottom to the top of mountains. Other topics include preparation for migration and the perils faced by migrating birds.

Simon, Seymour. *Ride the Wind: Airborne Journeys of Plants and Animals.* Illus. Elsa Warnick. New York: Harcourt: 1997. (Grades 4-8)

Simon, Seymour. *They Swim the Seas: The Mystery of Animal Migration.* Illus. Elsa Warnick. New York: Harcourt: 1998. (Grades 4-8)

Simon, Seymour. *They Walk the Earth: The Extraordinary Travels of Animal on Land.* Illus. Elsa Warnick. New York: Harcourt, 2000. (Grades 4-8)

Summary: This series on animal migration might be read aloud to introduce a migration unit. The sheer variety of the kinds of animals and habitats will be stimulating to students who may wish to choose one animal to research. A librarian may want to use these books to support an ongoing classroom unit on migration.

Arnold, Caroline. *Hawk Highway in the Sky: Watching Raptor Migration*. Illus. Robert Kruidenier. San Diego, CA: Harcourt Brace, 1997. (Grades 4-12)

Summary: This book features the HawkWatch International Raptor Migration Project in the Goshutes Mountains in Nevada. The text provides information about the project, facts about hawks and other raptors, and a picture of scientists at work. The illustrator has been a volunteer and photographer at the HawkWatch Project site for many years, and the photographs are from his collection. The author's acknowledgement includes information about where to write to learn about places to watch raptors. The Web site for HawkWatch listed in the book is outdated. Go to <http://www.hawkwatch.org> for information about the Hawkwatch organization and <http://www.hawkwatch.org/Research/Site%20Descriptions/Goshutes/goshutes_field_site.htm> for specific information about the Goshutes Mountain site.

Crenson, Victoria. *Horseshoe Crabs and Shorebirds: the Story of a Food Web*. Illus. Annie Cannon, New York: Marshall Cavendish, 2003. (Grades 4-12)

Summary: This book combines two stories. The first involves the annual journey of hundreds of thousands of horseshoe crabs from Delaware Bay to the shore to lay eggs. The second is the migration of South American birds, who depend on a rest and food stop in Delaware Bay on their way to the Arctic Circle. The connection is the horseshoe crab eggs, which provide the midjourney feast for over a million birds each year. The horseshoe crab population is shrinking, accompanied by a similar decline in bird migration through Delaware Bay. An author's note mentions the decline of both populations and possible reasons for the decreases. Use this book to demonstrate the nature of food webs and the fragility of the balance in such systems.

Lasky, Katherine. *Monarch*. Illus. Christopher Knight. New York: Harcourt Brace, 1993.

Summary: Lasky and Knight document the lives of monarch butterflies and their migration. The butterflies fly more than 2,000 miles while migrating, covering up to 80 miles per day. Lasky features El Rosario and Valle de Bravo, Mexico, and Pacific Grove, California, three places where monarch colonies migrate to in the winter annually, highlighting efforts to protect the known colony sites. The text acknowledges the fact that some migration routes and colony sites are still undiscovered and discusses the difficulty of tracking butterflies as they migrate.

Hiscock, Bruce. *The Big Caribou Herd: Life in the Arctic National Wildlife Refuge*. Honesdale, PA: Boyds Mills Press, 2003.

Summary: While this book focuses on the migration of the Porcupine Caribou herd, it also highlights the other animals of the Arctic National Refuge. The reader learns about wolves, muskoxen, polar bears and others. The author includes animal notes, a graph of the caribou yearly cycle, and an author's note at the end of the book.

Miller, Debbie. *A Woolly Mammoth Journey*. Illus. Jon Van Zyle. Boston: Little, Brown, 2001. (Grades 4-8)

Summary: *A Wooly Mammoth Journey* imagines the travels of a family of woolly mammoth over the course of one year. The reader witnesses the birth of a new mammoth, the meeting between two mammoth families, and the daily life of mammoths in the prehistoric world. The mammoths face dangers from the rough landscape they cross as well as the predators of the time. *When Mammoths Walked the Earth*, by Caroline Arnold, and *Woolly Mammoth: Life, Death, and Rediscovery* by Windsor Chorlton (see annotations below), will provide additional details about mammoths.

Discussion Questions:

- Mammoths are close cousins to present day elephants. What parallels can you find between this story and the things you know about elephant behavior?

- Bold One dies as he falls down a slope after the ground collapses under him.

- Do you think the author had evidence from fossils that a mammoth died this way? Why do you believe this? Did the author invent this theory to add drama to the story? Is it reasonable to assume that the ground on the edge of a cliff or hill could crumble under the feet of a mammoth? Upon what do you base your opinion?

Activities:

- Use this book with *When Mammoths Walked the Earth* and *Woolly Mammoth: Life, Death, and Rediscovery* to learn more about mammoths. Individual students or small groups might make a model of a woolly mammoth or a prehistoric landscape, complete with mammoths and other prehistoric species.

- Compare and contrast the lives, daily habits, and behavior of modern day elephants with those of mammoths.

- Students can research current theories about the causes of extinction of prehistoric species. Scientists disagree about these theories. Have students debate the various theories or write persuasive essays defending one theory.

- Create a map of mammoth fossils and remains found around the world.

Book Links: Mammoths

Arnold, Caroline. *When Mammoths Walked the Earth*. Illus. Laurie Caple. New York: Clarion, 2002. (Grades 4-12)

Summary: Arnold begins with the Ice Age and the first mammoths, discusses mammoths and their relatives, mammoth fossils, early man's interaction with mammoths, and ends with the last mammoths. The chapters are short, but packed with facts. One of the most interesting discussions is the 1997 discovery of the complete body of an adult mammoth frozen in the ground. Named after the hunters who discovered it, the Jarkov mammoth is preserved by storage in an ice cave so that it can melt gradually, allowing scientists to study it without decomposition. Students will wish to find out more about the Jarkov mammoth.

Windsor, Chorlton. *Wooly Mammoth: Life, Death, and Rediscovery*. New York: Scholastic, 2001. (Grades 4-12)

Summary: This book includes general information about life on the tundra, the age of mammoths, different types of mammoths, and mammoth finds. The bulk of the book is a detailed diary of the Jarkov Expedition and the subsequent and continuing study of the remains of the Jarkov mammoth. The details of the long, difficult process of cutting the huge block of permafrost out and transporting it to the ice cave, where it now resides, is fascinating. The author discusses the ongoing research made possible by the highly preserved specimen, and the debates over the controversial possibilities of cloning the mammoth or using the frozen sperm to crossbreed it with an Asian elephant. The bibliography lists museums, Web sites, and books for further information. A map of major mammoth finds completes the book. *Wooly Mammoth* is the perfect source for students intrigued by the mammoths. High school ethics classes will find fodder for debates about cloning or reviving extinct species in this book.

Book Links: Debbie Miller

Miller, Debbie S. *Arctic Lights, Arctic Nights*. Illus. Jon Van Zyle. New York, Walker, 2003. (Grades 4-12)

Summary: Inspired by questions from schoolchildren about the dynamics of light in Alaska, this author and illustrator team created a book that clearly shows the seasonal variations in light and temperature in the Fairbanks, Alaska area. Each page has a band of light and dark at the top of the page, depicting a specific 24-hour day. Below the band of light, the author lists the date, sunrise and sunset times, hours of daylight, and average high and low temperatures for that date. The main text and illustrations feature animal activity and the quality of light common to that time of year. A glossary of terms includes alpenglow (the red or pink tint seen on snow-covered mountains near sunrise or sunset) and other terms that may be unfamiliar.

Miller, Debbie S. *A Polar Bear Journey*. Illus. Jon Van Zyle. Boston, MA: Little, Brown, 1997. (Grades 4-7)

Summary: In November, a pregnant polar bear searches for a place to build her winter den. She dozes until January, when her two cubs are born. In late March, the family begins to go outside and leaves the den for good in April. The mother bear goes about the business of raising the cubs and teaching them to hunt. While the mother polar bear will stay with her cubs for two years, this account ends after the first year, when the bears get ready to den up for the winter. A page of polar bear facts is included at the end of the book.

Miller, Debbie S. *Disappearing Lake: Nature's Magic in Denali National Park*. Illus. Jon Van Zyle. New York: Walker, 1997. (Grades 4-8)

Summary: Disappearing Lake is a vernal lake, located in Alaska's Denali National Park, one of many lakes created annually by snowmelt and spring rains. As the summer progresses, these temporary lakes dry up. Many creatures visit these water systems during the spring and summer. In *Disappearing Lake*, the reader views animals as they visit the lake and the changes in the lake as the summer progresses. Several pages of "field notes" on the various animals are included at the end of the book, as well as an author's note.

Miller, Debbie S. *Flight of the Golden Plover: The Amazing Migration Between Hawaii and Alaska.* Illus. Daniel Van Zyle. Anchorage, AK: Alaska Northwest Books, 1996. (Grades 4-12)

Summary: The golden plover migrates each year between two very different ecosystems, Hawaii and Alaska. This book follows one plover family, beginning in Hawaii with the male's migration to Alaska, through mating and raising chicks, and ending as the fledglings making their independent migrations to Hawaii. The last page has a detailed report of facts about the plover.

 Animals

Lasky, Kathryn. *Shadows in the Dawn: The Lemurs of Madagascar.* Illus. Christopher Knight. New York: Harcourt Brace, 1998. (Grades 4-12)

Summary: *Shadows in the Dawn* features the behavior and history of lemurs, highlighting the danger posed to lemurs by destruction of Madagascar's wild habitats. The reader follows along with researcher Alison Jolly as she and others study the lemurs of Madagascar, which she has been observing for thirty years. The afterword gives an outdated address for Wildlife Preservation Trust International, now called Wildlife Trust, which is currently at <http://www.wpti.org/>.

Discussion Questions:

- Learning about dinosaurs bigger than her living room astonished Alison Jolly, and she became a scientist in order to be astonished regularly. What astonishes you? Do you like the feeling of astonishment? How could you choose a career that would keep astonishing you? Give some examples of astonishing careers.

- The lemur named Aunt Agatha changed researchers perceptions about which were the dominant members of lemur society. Why do you think scientists had formerly believed that the males were the dominant members of the troop? What did Alison have to observe to prove her theory?

Activities:

- Students can research the different species of lemur and make posters illustrating their physical characteristics, eating habits, and family groups.

- Have students go to the Wildlife Trust Web site. Wildlife Trust publishes an interesting educational newsletter, *The Wild Ones*, both in print and online. Students can explore this site and read the newsletter in the computer lab or library.

Book Links: Animals

Ryder, Joanne. *Jaguar in the Rain Forest*. Illus. Michael Rothman. New York: Morrow, 1996. (Grades 4-7)

Ryder, Joanne. *Shark in the Sea*. Illus. Michael Rothman. New York: Morrow, 1997. (Grades 4-7)

Summary: In each of these stories, a child imagines that he becomes the animal featured. The child appears on only the first and last pages, as by the second page he has become the animal. He spends a day in the body of the animal and then, returns to himself at the end of the book. It is an interesting concept, one that might lead to discussion about what it would be like to be an animal. Either of these books would be effective as a writing prompt in which students choose an animal to "become" in a story of their own.

London, Jonathan. *Panther: Shadow of the Swamp*. Illus. Paul Morin. Cambridge, MA: Candlewick, 2001. (Grades 4-12)

Summary: The Florida panther is an endangered species, threatened by loss of habitat and genetic deficiencies caused by inbreeding in such a small population. This introduction to the world of the panther is the story of one day's hunt. *Panther* would be appropriate for study of the poetic language used as well as for prompting interest in endangered species in general, and the panther specifically.

London, Jonathan. *Phantom of the Prairie: Year of the Black Footed Ferret*. Illus. Barbara Bush. San Francisco, CA: Sierra Club Books, 1998. (Grades 4-12)

Summary: The black-footed ferret is the most rare mammal in North America. Once believed to be extinct, one colony of the ferrets survived in a prairie dog town near Meeteetse, Wyoming. Disease reduced this one remaining colony to eighteen animals before scientists removed them to a captive breeding program. The breeding program has been successful, and colonies are thriving in the wild in several areas. London follows a wild black-footed ferret mother through a year as she raises her young. Information about the black-footed ferret is included at the end of the narrative.

Bonners, Susan. *Hunter in the Snow: The Lynx*. New York: Little, Brown, 1994.

Summary: The lynx is one of the shyest members of the cat family. Bonners details a year in the life of a female lynx. The pastel illustrations depict the lynx hunting, raising kittens, and other details of daily life. The lynx is heavily dependent on its main food source, the snowshoe hare. The text discusses the effect huge annual fluctuations in the hare population have on the lynx's ability to survive.

Facklam, Margery. *Spiders and Their Web Sites*. Illus. Alan Male. Boston, MA: Little, Brown, 2001. (Grades 4-12)

Summary: Twelve two-page spreads feature eleven kinds of spiders plus the daddy long legs, which is neither a spider nor an insect but a close cousin to both. Along with the more typical tarantula and black widow, Facklam includes purse spiders, fishing spiders, spitting spiders, cellar spiders, and other unusual varieties. A glossary and bibliography are included.

Simon, Seymour. *Spiders*. New York: HarperCollins, 2003. (Grades 4-12)

Summary: Simon provides a basic introduction to spiders, illustrated with large, clear photographs. *Spiders* is useful as a read aloud to introduce a spider unit or just for the delicious fun of learning about creepy things! The basic spider facts will provide a good base of knowledge to begin a study of spiders. Many kinds of spiders appear in the photographs, but the captions do not specifically identify each spider. This may prompt students to look for books that deal with specific types of spiders, such as, Christina Wilsdon's *National Audubon Society First Field Guide: Insects*, or Facklam's *Spiders and Their Web Sites*.

Froman, Nan. *What's That Bug?* Illus. Julian Mulock. New York: Little, Brown, 2001. (Grades 4-12)

Summary: Froman and Mulock present several pages of information about each of the nine most familiar orders of insects. The text is not a narrative, but consists of brief paragraphs and captions for the pictures. Students will enjoy browsing through the pictures while learning about insect classifications. The style is similar to Dorling Kindersley's Eyewitness books, but illustrated with detailed drawings rather than photographs.

 Scientists at Work

Dingus, Lowell, and Mark Norell. *Searching for Velociraptor*. New York: HarperCollins, 1996. (Grades 4-12)

Summary: This photo essay tells of the 1991 expedition to Mongolia to search for fossils of velociraptor, a dog-sized carnivorous dinosaur. The paleontologists hoped to follow in the footsteps of the famous explorer and naturalist, Roy Chapman Andrews, who first discovered both protoceratops and velociraptor in Mongolia in the 1920s. The authors provide a clear picture of the difficulties they faced on their search, even with modern day conveniences that Andrews's exploration team lacked. Older students may be inspired to find more information about the velociraptor, featured inaccurately in the film *Jurassic Park*. Other topics for research include Roy Chapman Andrews or paleontology.

Jackson, Donna M. *The Wildlife Detectives: How Forensic Scientists Fight Crimes Against Nature.* Illus. Wendy Shattil and Bob Rozinski. Boston, MA: Houghton Mifflin, 2000. (Grades 4-12)

Summary: The narrative in this book is the story of the poaching of Charger, a famous bull elk from Yellowstone National Park. The National Park Service and United States Fish and Wildlife Service teams, assisted by the Fish and Wildlife Forensics Lab in Oregon, worked together to find the poacher and prosecute him for his crime. Between episodes of the main story, "Wild Files," designed to look like file folders, present many facts about environmental issues and laws, wildlife forensics labs, poaching worldwide, ivory, eagles, and other related subjects.

Montgomery, Sy. *The Snake Scientist.* Illus. Nic Bishop. New York: Houghton Mifflin, 1999. (Grades 4-12)

Summary: Bob Mason, a zoologist at Oregon State University, spends about six weeks each year in Manitoba, Canada at the Narcisse Wildlife Management Area. The area contains three large snake pits, where thousands of red-sided garter snakes spend the winter underground in limestone caves. In the spring, they pour out of the ground, mate, then, go off to the marshes for the summer. Mason, whose nickname is the Snake Scientist, has studied these snakes for many years. He discovered that snakes use chemicals called pheromones to communicate with one another. This is a fascinating book, for both the insight into scientific studies and methods, and for the many pictures of snakes in huge bunches.

Book Links: Sy Montgomery

Montgomery, Sy. *The Tarantula Scientist.* Illus. Nic Bishop. Boston, MA: Houghton Mifflin, 2004. (Grades 4-12)

Montgomery, Sy. *The Man-Eating Tigers of Sundarbans.* Illus. Eleanor Briggs. Boston, MA: Houghton Mifflin, 2001. (Grades 4-12)

Salmansohn, Pete, and Stephen W. Kress. *Saving Birds: Heroes Around the World.* Gardiner, ME: Tilbury House, 2003. (Grades 4-12)

Summary: *Saving Birds* contains six stories of people all over the world working to save endangered birds. The birds included in this book are the common murres in California, lesser kestrels in Israel, black-necked cranes in China, hornbills in Malaysia, quetzals in Mexico, and black robins in New Zealand. Each section contains an essay and pictures detailing the bird's history, the reasons for its endangerment, and efforts to protect or save the species. Addresses and Web sites are included for readers who wish to learn more about one of the birds.

Arnosky, Jim. *Watching Desert Wildlife*. Washington DC: National Geographic, 1998. (Grades 4-12)

Summary: In *Watching Desert Wildlife*, Arnosky travels to the southwestern United States to study the wildlife of the desert. The text focuses on how to watch wildlife safely and successfully without disturbing the animals or the environment. On each page, the author sprinkles facts about the animals, along with tips for finding that particular animal. Arnosky's *Watching Water Birds* and *Following the Coast* are similar titles. The extensive *Crinkleroot* series features information in a folksy field guide format.

Book Links: Jim Arnosky

Arnosky, Jim. *Field Trips: Bug Hunting, Animal Tracking, Bird-watching, Shore Walking with Jim Arnosky*. New York: HarperCollins, 2002. (Grades 4-12)

Arnosky, Jim. *Watching Water Birds*. Washington DC: National Geographic, 1997. (Grades 4-7)

Arnosky, Jim. *Crinkleroot's Nature Almanac*. New York: Simon and Schuster, 1999.

Arnosky, Jim. *Following the Coast*. New York: HarperCollins, 2004. (Grades 4-7)

Arnosky, Jim. *Crinkleroot's Guide to Knowing Animal Habitats*. New York: Simon and Schuster, 1997. (Grades 4-12)

Arnosky, Jim. *Wild and Swampy*. New York: HarperCollins, 2000. (Grades 4-8)

Book Links: Scientists at Work

Lewin, Ted, and Betsy. *Elephant Quest*. New York: HarperCollins, 2000. (Grades 4-12)

Summary: This book, illustrated with watercolor paintings and sketches, chronicles the Lewins' four-day stay in the Moremi Reserve located in the Okavango Delta of Botswana. They visit during the rainy season in April in hopes of seeing some of the 70,000 elephants who live in the Reserve. After four days of searching, during which they see many other animals, the elephants finally make an appearance. The book may lead to discussion of proper behavior when viewing animals in the wild. The authors have included two pages of elephant facts. The Lewins have also observed gorillas and documented their experience in *Gorilla Walk*.

Lewin, Ted, and Betsy. *Gorilla Walk*. New York: Lothrop, Lee and Shepard, 1999. (Grades 4-8)

Swineburn, Stephen R. *The Woods Scientist*. Illus. Susan C. Morse. Boston, MA: Houghton Mifflin, 2002. (Grades 4-12)

Weather

Simon, Seymour. *Hurricanes*. New York: HarperCollins, 2003. (Grades 4-12)

Summary: Simon's series on natural disasters includes *Earthquakes*, *Storms*, *Tornados*, *Volcanoes*, and *Wildfires*, along with this title. The activities listed for this volume can be adapted for use with any of the books in this series. In *Hurricanes*, Simon explains what hurricanes are and why they are considered the worst kind of storm. He clearly describes the meaning of the hurricane scale, Category One through Category Five. The text includes an examination of how weather forecasters predict hurricanes and the development of the early warning system that has saved lives in recent years. Simon lists some of the most deadly hurricanes in history. He concludes with an essay on preparations for hurricanes and instructions for dealing with the aftermath of the storms.

Activities:

Hurricanes and other disasters are fascinating to students, but misconceptions about them are frequent, partly due to hearsay, urban legend, and folklore. The objective for this activity is to activate students' prior knowledge and help them learn to modify their knowledge base when science proves their information out of date or faulty. Before reading the book aloud, have students brainstorm what they know about hurricanes. Use butcher paper and a marker to record students' ideas. Do not attempt to correct misperceptions or resolve conflicting ideas—simply record all student contributions. On a second sheet of butcher paper, write students' questions about hurricanes. Next, read the book aloud. Have students listen for information that confirms or disagrees with their ideas or provides answers to their questions. Stop when necessary to correct information on the charts. Using a second color, underline information confirmed by the text, correct inaccuracies, and add details to the first list. Record answers to questions on the second list. If desired, extend the lesson using any of the following activities:

- Add a third sheet of butcher paper for student responses. They can record their impressions of the text and discuss the information learned.

- Students can take the facts learned and make posters about hurricanes. Small groups could each take a different aspect of the text, create a poster and share the completed posters with the class. Groups could present their poster orally, perhaps to another class studying the same topic.

- Simon's text may not answer all of the questions brainstormed in the first lesson. Further research in the library will help students fill in the blanks.

- Students may find it difficult to accept the information in the book. They may doubt Simon's accuracy or believe the folklore they learned as a child rather than the facts he presents. This is a perfect opportunity to discover that not all information is equal, and to learn to look at the authority of the author or source. Web pages are an excellent place to find information—but a wonderful place to find misinformation as well. Books, too, can be mistaken or out of date. Students can consult other sources to prove or deny their theories or the information in Simon's book.

- In this book, the role of weather forecasters is very important. Students may be interested in learning more about weather forecasting. If possible, invite a meteorologist to visit and speak with students about weather, storms, and forecasting.

Chapter $\boxed{4}$

History: Using Fiction and Nonfiction Picture Books in Social Studies Units

Many picture books are well suited for use in history class. For some eras, there are many books to choose from; for others, there are relatively few. The wars seem to take much of our attention, and some wars receive more emphasis than others, as is probably true in general adult literature as well as children's books. In the world of picture books, the issues of the Civil War and World War II receive much attention, while the American Revolutionary War and World War I seem relatively underrepresented. The Vietnam War era and the Gulf War are nearly invisible, but the Civil Rights movement in the United States is frequently chronicled, especially the life and work of Dr. Martin Luther King. Fewer picture books cover the women's rights movement and general human and civil rights struggles around the world. Ancient history and civilizations have received some attention, as well. Only a very few books deal with more specific historical events, such as the great influenza epidemic of 1918 or the Oklahoma City Bombing of 1994. World exploration and colonization are frequently covered in biographies, listed in another chapter of this book. The books that follow appear in roughly chronological order, grouped together by era and theme.

Historical picture books can be used in a variety of ways. A simple reading of one of these books, followed by student questions and discussion, may spark interest in the topic by making the history more real to the student. Facts are less boring when students perceive the human emotion, the sacrifices made, and the life-changing impact historical events had on everyday life. In addition, many of these stories show a small piece of the bigger picture, leaving many questions in the student's mind. When students have an emotional connection to history, research becomes passionate, rather than just another teacher driven report. When a student is allowed to choose a topic and investigate it based upon what she learned in the picture book, she will be more motivated to find information and share it with others. The difficulty of helping students develop research questions and theses becomes easier when they find a topic truly interesting.

The history books featured here are a wonderful place to begin. The more you use picture books in your history lessons, the more readily you will spot them as you browse the shelves of your local library or bookstore.

 # Ancient History and Civilization

Major, John S. *The Silk Route: 7,000 Miles of History.* Illus Stephen Fieser. New York: HarperCollins, 1995. (Grades 4-12)

Summary: The Silk Road was a trade route linking China with Europe, the Middle East, and Western Asia. Trade caravans traveled the route as early as 100 BC and continued through the fifteenth century, but the route reached its peak of importance during the Tang Dynasty in China, A.D. 618-906. *The Silk Route*, set in A.D. 700, provides a glimpse of the myriad of goods traded and the hardships of travel through the harsh deserts and mountains. The reader follows one trade caravan, which begins in Chang'an, China, and ends in Byzantium. Additional details are included in an author's note at the end of the book.

Winters, Kay. *Voices of Ancient Egypt.* Illus. Barry Moser. Washington, D.C.: National Geographic, 2003. (Grades 4-12)

Summary: Naturally, the pharaohs, mummies, and pyramids of ancient Egypt receive the lion's share of students' attention. *Voices of Ancient Egypt* focuses on the ordinary people who worked and lived in the times of the pyramids. The reader meets a wide variety of workers, including a pyramid builder, a birdnetter, a scribe, an embalmer, and a farmer. The illustrations depict each person on the job, accompanied by a first person, free verse poem describing his work and place in the culture. The book concludes with a bibliography and a historical note with additional information about each worker.

Book Links: Ancient History and Civilization

Chrisp, Peter. *Ancient Rome Revealed.* New York: DK Publishing, 2003. (Grades 4-12)

Collard, Sneed. *1,000 Years Ago on Planet Earth.* Illus Jonathan Hunt. Boston, MA: Houghton Mifflin, 1999. (Grades 4-12)

Tanaka, Shelley. *Secrets of the Mummies: Uncovering the Bodies of Ancient Egyptians.* Illus. Greg Ruhl. New York: Hyperion/Madison Press, 1999. (Grades 4-12)

Tanaka, Shelley. *The Buried City of Pompeii: What it was Like When Vesuvius Exploded.* Illus. Greg Ruhl. New York: Hyperion/Madison Press, 1997. (Grades 4-12)

Curlee, Lynn. *Seven Wonders of the Ancient World.* New York, Atheneum, 2002. (Grades 4-12)

The Middle Ages

Tanaka, Shelley. *In the Time of Knights: The Real-life Story of History's Greatest Knight.* Illus. Greg Ruhl. New York: Hyperion/Madison Press, 2000. (Grades 4-12)

Summary: The text follows William Marshal (1152-1219) from age six until his death. The reader learns of his training for knighthood, his strength in battle, and weakness in the scholarly pursuits expected of knights. Despite his faults, he eventually became one of the most important knights in England. Marshal governed England while Richard the Lion-Heart fought in the Crusades and later, became regent for the young King Henry III. While the narrative reads like an action-packed biography, much of the focus is on the customs of the time, with extensive sidebars containing historical background.

Book Links: The Middle Ages

Aliki. *A Medieval Feast.* New York: Harper & Row, 1986

Nikola-lisa, W. *Till Year's Good End: A Calendar of Medieval Labors.* Illus. Christopher Manson. New York: Atheneum, 1997.

The Early Modern World

Fisher, Leonard Everett. *The Tower of London.* New York: MacMillan, 1987.

Summary: The Tower of London is a fortress that includes towers, apartments, crypts, a church, a great hall, and guardhouses. This history of the Tower of London chronicles the building and remodeling of the facility and highlights the changing uses of the castle through the centuries. Fisher relates thirteen sensational incidents from the history of the Tower of London, including imprisonments, executions, marriages, and political wrangling.

Activities:

- Students can take a virtual tour of the Tower of London at <http://www.camelotintl.com/tower_site/index.html>. This is an official site, created in association with the Yeoman Warders of the Tower. It includes several narrated tours as well as history, maps, and photographs.

- Students could research one of the thirteen famous events mentioned in the text or discover other infamous prisoners or incidents in the Tower's history.

- Have students map the Tower of London and the surrounding area, including Tower Hill, the site of many executions.

- The Tower of London will pair well with *The Ravenmaster's Secret* by Elvira Woodruff, which tells a story about the son of the Yeoman Warder Ravenmaster. Students reading *The Ravenmaster's Secret* will appreciate the raven section of the Tower of London Web site mentioned above.

Mannie, Celeste Davidson. *The Queen's Progress: An Elizabethan Alphabet.* Illus. Bagram Ibatoulline. New York: Viking, 2003. (Grades 4-12)

Summary: During her 44-year reign, Queen Elizabeth I spent each summer on a "progress," which was a vacation and a chance to connect with her subjects. Her entourage included hundreds of courtiers and attendants and an enormous amount of baggage. The Queen's possessions alone filled 400 carts. *The Queen's Progress* works on many levels. It is an illuminated alphabet with a series of rhyming verses, a view of the history and culture of England in the 1560s, and a biography of Elizabeth I, all packaged into a richly illustrated picture book.

 # The American Revolution

Kirkpatrick, Katherine. *Redcoats and Petticoats.* Illus Ronald Himler. New York: Holiday House, 1999. (Grades 4-12)

Summary: From 1778-1784, the Setauket Spy Ring on Long Island helped to carry critical information from British occupied New York City to patriots in Connecticut. When Redcoats imprison his father and take over the family home, Thomas Strong and his mother move the family to a small cottage across the bay. Mother uses her clothesline as a signaling device as part of the spy ring. Thomas is an unknowing link in the spy ring, rowing out to see if a whaleboat is in the bay and thereby giving his mother the information to send via her clothesline message service. Thomas's father is a captive on the prison ship *Jersey.* With the help of his Tory relatives and a boatload of vegetables, Thomas and his mother are able to buy Father's freedom. Historical notes, maps, and an explanation of the spy ring in action accompany the story.

Discussion Questions:

- As you read the book aloud to students, take time to stop and have students infer what is happening and predict what might happen next. Thomas slowly figures out that there is method to Mother's apparent madness. Older students will figure it out before Thomas does, and some may be able to decipher the clothesline code as well.

- Why did Thomas's mother decide to use him without telling him what she was doing and why? Would it be easier or harder to do the task if you knew? If you had been Thomas's mother, would you have told him? Do you think it was easier for Thomas to face the Redcoats without knowing why he was out rowing?

- What were Thomas's feelings about the tall Redcoat who took over his house and then kept taking the fish he caught?

Activities:

- Use this book to introduce the value of oral history. Have students interview an older person about an event from their childhood or lifetime. While not every story will be as dramatic as a spy ring, many could tell of something an ancestor did during a war or a homesteading or immigration story from family history. Alternatively, students could ask about memories of a significant national event such as the assassination of President Kennedy or an aspect of everyday life, such as, how milk got to the dinner table.

- Research the prison ship *Jersey*. The author tells us a little about the ship, including the amazing fact that eleven thousand men died on the *Jersey*. Questions could include how many men were imprisoned there and for how long, the size of the ship, and the number of prisoners who were bought off the ship, as Thomas's father was. Research could also include some facts about the Prison Ship Martyrs' Monument in Fort Greer Park, Brooklyn.

- Research the Setauket Spy Ring in further detail. Find out how many other spy rings were in operation, and how historians have documented their work. Consult the sources mentioned in the text.

- This is a good opportunity to study codes of all kinds. The Navajo code talkers in World War II are one possible topic. Developing a code for an imaginary spy ring and implementing it to plan a surprise party or other school function would be a fun class project.

Turner, Ann. *Katie's Trunk*. Illus. Ron Himler. New York: MacMillan, 1992. (Grades 4-12)

Summary: Katie's family lives in Boston. As Tories, they are loyal to the King of England. Former friends and neighbors, who are now Rebels, come to ransack Katie's house. Her family hides in the woods, but Katie returns to the house, angry and ready to protect their belongings. Once there, she realizes she is in danger and hides in her mother's wedding trunk. A Rebel boy opens the trunk and discovers her while looking for treasures, but does not report her presence. He calls the other Rebels away when Tory soldiers arrive outside, saving her from capture. She realizes that the boy had left "one seam of goodness" there when he prevented the rebels from finding her in the trunk.

Discussion Questions:

- Katie's mother talked about "sewing a straight seam for goodness sake" and later Katie realizes that the boy had left a "seam of goodness" when he prevented her discovery in the trunk. What do you think this means? How could it apply to your life? Is there a way to preserve goodness in bad situations? Is anyone completely bad, or is there a bit of goodness in everyone?

- Friends and families served on opposite sides in both the Revolutionary and Civil Wars. What would you have done if your friends all joined one side and your convictions made you their enemy?

Activities:

- Katie's family was Tory, but many of her friends and neighbors were Revolutionaries. Students can investigate the Tories. Find out how many Loyalists or Tories lived in the colonies and how they functioned.

- This text mentions the Boston Tea Party. After researching the incident, students could choose to stage a debate, design a flyer advertising the need for volunteers, write a Tory newspaper article reporting on the horrible deed, or give a PowerPoint presentation outlining the facts and myths of the Boston Tea Party.

Book Links: The American Revolution

Turner, Ann. *When Mr. Jefferson Came to Philadelphia: What I Learned of Freedom, 1776.* Illus. Mark Hess. New York: HarperCollins, 2003. (Grades 4-12)

Summary: In this short, simple book, Turner uses poetic language to tell the story of Ned, whose mother ran the boardinghouse where Thomas Jefferson stayed while writing the Declaration of Independence. The story is not a deep discussion of Jefferson's life or accomplishments, but a vignette of one boy's experience in thinking about the issues of the time. Is Jefferson committing treason? Is freedom from England a worthy cause? Is revolution treasonous by definition?

Winnick, Karen B. *Sybil's Night Ride.* Honesdale, PA: Boyd's Mills Press, 2000. (Grades 4-12)

Summary: Sybil Luddington was a Revolutionary War heroine. On April 26, 1777, she rode forty miles in the rain to muster her father's troops to fight the British, who were burning the town of Danbury, Connecticut. Thanks to her efforts, the regiment was able to meet with others and push the British back until they fled by boat to New York City. *Sybil's Night Ride* provides a good counterpoint to the more famous ride of Paul Revere and makes students aware that women, too, participated in the Revolutionary War.

Kroll, Steven. *The Boston Tea Party.* Illus by Peter Fiore. New York: Holiday House, 1998. (Grades 4-12)

Peacock, Louise. *Crossing the Delaware: A History in Many Voices.* Illus Walter Lyon Krudop. New York: Atheneum, 1998. (Grades 4-12)

 # The Civil War

Polacco, Patricia. *Pink and Say.* New York: Philomel, 1994.

Summary: Patricia Polacco's great great grandfather Sheldon Russell Curtis (Say) fought on the Union side in the Civil War. Pinkus Aylee (Pink) was an African American Union Soldier. Pink was separated from his unit when he found Say injured and left for dead in Confederate territory. Pink took Say to his mother, Moe Moe Bay, on a nearby deserted plantation. As Say healed, the two boys became friends. When Confederate marauders came to the plantation, Moe Moe Bay hid the boys, but she did not survive. Confederate troops eventually captured the boys and imprisoned them in Andersonville, the worst of the Confederate prisoner of war camps.

This is a many-layered story, dealing with issues including, but not limited to: slaves who learned to read and poor white boys who did not; the harsh realities of war, death, and destruction; the different treatment of blacks and whites by the Confederate soldiers; the Confederate prisoner of war camps; and the innocent lives taken by war. It is an emotional tale, which often moves adults to tears. The fact that it is also a true story based on oral history makes it even more poignant. Be sure to read this one to yourself before reading it to students!

Discussion Questions: This book will raise many questions in student's minds. See the activities section for suggestions on eliciting and using those questions.

- Say learns that Pink bears the last name of his master, because "when you owned, you ain't got no name of your own." What do you think it would be like not to have a family name? How does your last name help define you to the world and to yourself? If you were a freed slave, would you keep the master's name or choose one of your own? What might your choice be?

- One of the illustrations shows only two hands clasped surrounded by white space. Why did Polacco choose to leave out the background? You will notice that she uses white space in all of her books. What do you think that technique does for the illustrations?

Activities:

- As you read this book, pause and ask students to write down the questions they are thinking about as they listen to the story. You will have found natural places to pause as you read the story to yourself in preparation. You can use these student generated questions in a variety of ways: have a class discussion; reread the book, stopping at the same places to discuss the questions the students wrote down the first time; or have students discuss their questions in small groups.

- Research Andersonville camp. What gave it the reputation as the worst Confederate camp? What happened to the people there? How many were imprisoned there, and how many survived?

Turner, Ann. *Drummer Boy.* Illus. Mark Hess. New York: HarperCollins, 1998. (Grades 4-12)

Summary: After listening to a speech by President Lincoln, a thirteen-year-old boy runs away from home to join the Union Army. He becomes a drummer boy. In one of the battles, the drummer boy holds the hand of a wounded soldier as he dies on the battlefield. As the story ends, the boy wishes he could tell the President how Lincoln's "great, sad eyes made me go and see things no boy should ever see."

Discussion Questions:

- President Lincoln's speech inspired this boy to go to war, against the wishes of his family. Can you think of someone in today's world who could inspire you to take a risk to help a cause, your school, or country?

- What do you think the boy felt about President Lincoln after he had experienced the war? He says that he has seen "things no boy should ever see." Do you think he resents the President for inspiring him to go and see these things?

- The drummer boy was thirteen. How old were the regular soldiers in the Civil War? Is the age limit for the United States armed forces different today? What is the minimum age for soldiers in other countries? How old should you have to be to go to war?

Activities:

- Research the role of the drummer boy in the Civil War. Were they required to fight? What happened when they were in the middle of battle and could not escape? What were the cadences they used to call out the commands to the army?

- Find a Civil War reenactment group and ask to observe a reenactment. This would make a very exciting field trip. Taking part in a reenactment might be an option for some students.

- Have students pick one battle of the Civil War to research. Students could choose to diagram the flow of the battle; do a PowerPoint presentation on the battle; show the battle from the point of view of a drummer boy, a commander, or a soldier or write an essay describing the battle.

Book Links: The Civil War

Lewin, Ted. *Red Legs: A Drummer Boy of the Civil War.* New York: HarperCollins, 2001. (Grades 4-12)

Summary: *Red Legs* is a clever mix of history and present-day reality, based on a real drummer boy, Stephen Benjamin Bartow. Stephen served in the fourteenth regiment of Brooklyn called Red Legs because of the color of their uniforms. In this story, Stephen is shot and dies. When his father's hand reaches down to help him up, the reader realizes that this Stephen is participating in a present-day Civil War reenactment. The author's note at the end puts it all in perspective. *Red Legs* would serve as an introduction to research on reenactment groups and their purposes or interest students in researching the real Stephen Bartow or another Civil War soldier. Students could locate and observe reenactment groups focusing on different periods. Plan a field trip to a museum such as the Plimoth Colony, where staff and volunteers play the parts of people from that time.

Ransom, Candice. *The Promise Quilt.* Illus. Ellen Beier. New York: Walker 1999. (Grades 4-8)

Summary: Addie lives in an isolated area of the south during the Civil War. Her father goes to war to be General Lee's guide. Her mother is making a quilt as she waits for Father to come back from the war. In this rural setting, slavery is not evident, and the war seems remote. When Father does not return from the war, Addie's family struggles to find a way to remember and honor him. The schoolhouse accidentally burns down, and Addie's mother wants to rebuild the facility so the children can return to school after the war. Mother sends the quilt to a friend in the North, who raffles it to provide funds for books and building materials.

Slavery and the Underground Railroad

Lester, Julius. *From Slave Ship to Freedom Road*. Illus. Rod Brown. New York: Dial, 1998. (Grades 7-12)

Summary: Over the course of seven years, Rod Brown created thirty-six paintings depicting the history of slavery. Julius Lester and Rod Brown selected twenty of the paintings for this book. Lester's meditations accompany each painting. The paintings are powerful and stark and depict slavery in an unflinching manner. This book is not suitable for younger readers. The text includes historical narration, the imagined words of the people in the paintings, quotations, and Lester's personal thoughts. Lester poses many questions in the text, including "Imagination Exercises" targeted at African Americans, white Americans, and sometimes, both. The paintings themselves lead to many questions, and the text urges readers to think about the reality of slavery and the dangers of the attitudes that led to the institution of slavery. This book will be useful in history, art, and writing classes. The following general questions are designed to be used either after the entire book is read or with any picture in the collection.

Discussion Questions:

- What was the motivation for the artist to create these paintings?

- What kind of research did the artist have to do in order to paint these pictures well and make sure they were historically accurate?

- Examine the faces in any of the paintings. What are the people feeling? What are their lives like? How do their lives compare to your life?

Activities:

- Students can research the slave trade. Use the interest and questions generated by the book to help students focus on different aspects of slavery. Each student or group of students can choose a different painting and concentrate on one question that it poses for them. The final product could be a PowerPoint presentation, using artistic and photographic sources to illustrate the facts found during research.

- Julius Lester has written several books about slavery. His first book, *To Be a Slave*, combined historical perspectives and personal narratives of former slaves. He has also written two novels about slavery, *Long Journey Home* and *This Strange New Feeling*. Teachers can use one of these as a class reading assignment or choose excerpts to share with students. As an alternative, an individual student can explore these works as part of an assignment or for extra credit.

- Rod Brown and Julius Lester selected twenty of thirty-six paintings. See if you can find the other sixteen paintings. Look for other examples of Rod Brown's work.

Vaughan, Marcia. *The Secret to Freedom.* Illus. Larry Johnson. New York: Lee and Low, 2001. (Grades 4-12)

Summary: A ten-year-old girl listens to her Great Aunt Lucy tell the story of her youth as a slave. As young children, Lucy and her brother Albert remained on the plantation after the overseer sold their parents. In the years that follow, Albert and Lucy learn the messages hidden in quilt patterns and participate in helping runaway slaves. Lucy, who is lame, hangs out the quilts at the appropriate times, while Albert takes slaves on their first steps on the Underground Railroad. When the overseer begins to suspect Albert's involvement, he must run away himself, reluctantly leaving Lucy behind. Lucy gives Albert a quilt square as a remembrance. Lucy becomes a teacher and a wife, never knowing if Albert survived. One day she receives a letter containing the quilt square and a message from her brother. An extensive author's note explains the quilt code and gives definitions of the quilt patterns.

Discussion Questions:

- Why did Lucy pressure Albert to run away without her? Did that also put Lucy at risk from the overseer?

- What would you have done if you were Albert?

- Would you have been able to urge your brother to run away without you if you were in Lucy's position?

Activities:

- For many years, Lucy did not know if Albert escaped or died in his attempt to run away. Imagine you lost your parents and brother and had no reason to believe that you would ever see them again. Write a letter to send to your brother in case he is still alive. What will you tell him?

- Imagine you are Albert and have successfully made it to freedom. Write the letter you will send to try to find your sister.

- *The Secret to Freedom* presents the coded quilt messages as fact. Compare with *Under the Quilt of Night*, where Deborah Hopkinson notes that the existence of a quilt code for the Underground Railroad is unproven and debated by historians. Use the sources listed in both books and other resources to find out what historians believe today about the freedom quilts. After reading and researching, write a position paper telling what you believe to be true. Support your beliefs with examples and quotes from your sources.

Hopkinson, Deborah. *Under the Quilt of Night.* Illus. James E. Ransome. New York: Atheneum, 2001. (Grades 4-12)

Summary: *Under the Quilt of Night* is based on fact and legend about the Underground Railroad. A young girl and her companions escape from slavery and flee toward the Canadian border. Poetic language and luminous paintings depict the nights of running and hiding, the relief of finding refuge in safe houses, and the fear and hope felt on the journey. The author notes that the idea of quilts containing secret meanings for runaway slaves is controversial among historians, some of whom consider it legend rather than fact. Pair this title with Hopkinson's companion volume, *Sweet Clara and the Freedom Quilt*, and Vaughan's *The Secret to Freedom*.

Discussion Questions:

- Do you think these slaves made it to their final destination and freedom in the North?

- How does the author pack so much meaning into so few words? Show an example of a simple phrase that represents a much larger concept.

Activities:

- Do quilters assign meanings to patterns and colors in their quilts? Have students find out about the quilting process and the meanings behind some of the quilts. Invite a quilter to show her work and explain the symbolism behind some of the pieces. Students can research modern quilt designs and their meanings.

- Search the Internet for more information on the Underground Railroad, especially the family stories that add to our understanding of history. Create a Web quest about the Underground Railroad and stories of runaway slaves.

Book Links: Slavery and the Underground Railroad

Hopkinson, Deborah. *Sweet Clara and the Freedom Quilt*. Illus. James E. Ransome New York: Knopf, 1993. (Grades 4-8)

Summary: Clara is a seamstress in the Big House, which is a fairly good life for a slave, but she dreams of reuniting with her mother someday. When she hears the other slaves talking about wanting a map of the Underground Railroad to assist them in running away to freedom, she decides to make a map disguised as a quilt.

Lawrence, Jacob. *Harriet and the Promised Land*. New York: Simon and Schuster, 1993. (Grades 4-12)

Summary: Jacob Lawrence created a series of paintings honoring Harriet Tubman. In this book, the paintings are paired with poetic text to tell the story of Harriet Tubman's journeys to help runaway slaves along the Underground Railroad. *Harriet and the Promised Land* would be appropriate to use in a study of Jacob Lawrence's art or in a unit about slavery and the Underground Railroad. The text provides a good starting point for a research project on Harriet Tubman or the organization of the Underground Railroad.

Winter, Jeanette. *Follow the Drinking Gourd*. New York: Knopf, 1988. (Grades 4-12)

Summary: Peg Leg Joe was a legendary conductor on the Underground Railroad. Joe hired himself out to plantation owners as a handyman, made friends with the slaves, and taught them the "harmless" folk song, "Follow the Drinking Gourd." Hidden in the lyrics of the song were directions for finding the way to freedom. The legend says that Joe left tracks of his peg leg along the way so the slaves would know they were on the right path. An author's note includes details about the legend of Peg Leg Joe and the Underground Railroad, as well as the music and words for the song.

Rappaport, Doreen. *Freedom River*. Illus. Bryan Collier. New York: Hyperion, 2000. (Grades 4-12)

Summary: Freedom River refers to the Ohio River at Ripley, Ohio. In the days before the Civil War, the Ohio River separated Kentucky, a slave state, from the free state of Ohio. John Parker was a freed slave and businessman in Ripley, Ohio and was one of the most famous and active conductors on the Underground Railroad. He made many trips across the river to help slaves escape from Kentucky and continue on to safety. This tale tells of one such rescue.

Sanders, Scott Russell. *A Place called Freedom*. Illus. Thomas B. Allen. New York: Atheneum, 1997. (Grades 4-12)

Summary: In 1832, before the Civil War, a plantation owner frees his slaves, including the Starman family. The family travels north to Indiana, where they slowly build a successful life. In time, the father travels back to Tennessee to free relatives and friends, who join the community. When the community grows big enough to need a name, the townsfolk decide to name it Freedom. *A Place Called Freedom* was inspired by the true story of the founding of Lyles Station, Indiana.

Turner, Ann. *Nettie's Trip South*. Illus. Ronald Himler. New York: Simon and Schuster, 1987. (Grades 4-12)

Summary: Inspired by Ann Turner's great-great grandmother's diary, this book tells the story of Nettie, who goes on a trip into the South in 1859. Nettie begins the journey with no understanding of the reality of slavery. Her puzzlement is especially apparent when she learns that blacks are considered "no more than three-quarters of a person." To Nettie, blacks seem the same as whites except for the color of their skin. She witnesses a slave auction and is so horrified she becomes ill. Her response to the general living conditions of slaves and the spectacle of the auction is very moving.

Nolen, Jerdine. *Big Jabe*. Illus. Kadir Nelson. New York: Lothrop, Lee and Shepard, 2000. (Grades 4-8)

Summary: Big Jabe is an original tall tale. A slave on Simon Plenty's plantation finds a child floating down the river in a basket. She discovers that he is no ordinary child. He calls the fish out of the water when they are not biting, and grows into a man with the "strength of 50" in a single season. Big Jabe has a knack for making the slaves' lives a little better. When Mr. Plenty punishes a slave, the slave disappears overnight—gone to freedom. Students will find echoes of Harriet Tubman and Moses in this tale.

After the Civil War

Johnston, Tony. *The Wagon*. Illus. James E. Ransome. New York: Tambourine Books, 1996. (Grades 4-12)

Summary: A boy is born in Carolina, "but like all my family, birth to grave, my skin made me a slave." His father makes a wagon for the master. In the boy's imagination, the wagon becomes a chariot to carry the family away from slavery. As the Civil War begins, the boy is disillusioned and chops at the wagon's wheel, calling it a "chariot of false hope." He finds hope in the story of Abraham Lincoln chopping wood. When the war is over, the family does leave slavery in the wagon. The boy's feeling of deliverance is tempered with the news of Lincoln's death.

Discussion Questions:

- When the boy went with his father to deliver goods or pick up supplies, sometimes they delivered other slaves to auction. Imagine you were taking your friends, neighbors, or family to be sold. How would you feel? What would you be able to do about it?

- When an old man nearly died from a whipping, the boy cried and received a beating for crying. How would that feel? What would you do in that situation? Was there anything the boy could have done to help the old man?

- In the dedication, the author says, "I touch old wood. I touch old wounds." What do you think she meant? How does this statement relate to the story? There are several places where the text mentions the color or feel of wood. Look them over and think about the message the author wants the reader to understand.

- The Master inspected the wagon as he would a horse or a slave. Imagine you are a slave and someone is inspecting you to see if he might want to buy you. What would your thoughts be?

Activities:

- There are many examples of poetic language in this book. Have students choose a sentence from the story and write about the feeling generated by that statement. Have them describe the images it brings to mind and how the words connect to their own lives. For example: "We were scared. Who could see down Freedom's furrow?"

- What would life be like for freed slaves? Have you ever wanted something, but found that when you got it, you were not sure what to do with it?

- The author writes: "Then everything changed. The President wrote some words one day. We had gone to bed slaves. But we woke up free. . . But ol' Freedom dragged her feet, took her sweet time catching up to those words." Research the lives of slaves after slavery ended. How long did it take the plantation owners to give them their freedom?

- The owner gave this family the wagon and two mules, and they became farmers. How did other former slaves make their livings? Were they employed, and in what jobs? Did employers treat them fairly? Were freed slaves able to stay in the South? How long did it take them to earn enough money to own land?

- *The Wagon* is based on a painting by illustrator, James Ransome. The idea of making an entire story inspired by a single paining is intriguing. Have students choose a painting or piece of art and write a story about the people or events illustrated by the artwork.

- Ransome is a prolific illustrator. Teachers can share other picture books illustrated by Ransome. Students can research Ransome's life and work.

 # Westward Migration in the United States

Russell, Marion, adapted by Ginger Wadsworth. *Along the Santa Fe Trail: Marion Russell's Own Story.* Illus. James Watling. Morton Grove, IL: Albert Whitman, 1993. (Grades 4-12)

Summary: Marion Russell's book, *Land Of Enchantment,* is about her life and her experiences on the Santa Fe Trail, which she traveled five times. For this book, Ginger Wadsworth has adapted Russell's text in a picture book format, using Marion's words wherever possible. It tells of her first childhood trip on the Santa Fe Trail, with her widowed mother and her brother Will.

Johnston, Tony. *Sunsets of the West.* Illus. Ted Lewin. New York: GP Putnam's Sons, 2002. (Grades 4-8)

Summary: *Sunsets of the West* tells the tale of a family traveling in a covered wagon from New England to Missouri, and then, on to the Sierra Nevada area of California to settle. This book contains much detail about needing to wait days as buffalo herds cross the trail, passing graves of other travelers, losing animals, lightening the load, and other privations of the long journey. It ends with the successful building of a home and farm. This book would be a nice one to add to a unit on westward migration or the Oregon Trail, although this family branches off toward California rather than Oregon.

 # Exploration

Edwards, Judith. *The Great Expedition of Lewis and Clark.* Illus. Sally Wern Comport. New York: Farrar, Straus, Giroux, 2003. (Grades 4-12)

Summary: Edwards provides an account of the exploration done by Lewis and Clark and the Corps of Discovery, narrated by Reubin Field, one of the men selected for the Corps. Reubin Field was a real person; the author has imagined what his voice would have been like to create this oral retelling of the adventure. An afterword tells details about Reubin Field and his life after returning from the trip. For a different perspective on the Lewis and Clark Expedition, see *My Name is York*, the story of Captain Clark's slave, York, who accompanied his master on the trip.

Book Links: Exploration

Goodman, Joan Elizabeth. *Beyond the Sea of Ice: The Voyages of Henry Hudson*. Illus. Fernando Rangel. New York: Mikaya Press, 1999. (Grades 4-12)

Van Steenwyk, Elizabeth. *My Name is York*. Illus. Bill Farnsworth. Flagstaff, AZ: Northland Publishing, 1997. (Grades 4-12)

Curlee, Lynn. *Into the Ice: The Story of Artic Exploration*. Boston, MA: Houghton Mifflin, 1998. (Grades 4-12)

 # World War I

Foreman, Michael. *War Game*. New York: Arcade, 1993. (Grades 4-12)

Summary: In this story based on a true incident, members of an English soccer team "join up"—enlist as soldiers—and go to war to fight the Germans in World War I. On Christmas, troops from both sides leave their trenches, sing together, and play a game of soccer, in a brief respite from fighting. After the soccer game, the soldiers return to their respective trenches, and the war continues, with a difference. Now the enemy has a face. The illustrations are interspersed with pictures of posters and flyers used to recruit soldiers and bolster the war effort in England.

Discussion Questions:

- When the boys go to enlist, they each have different feelings about joining up. If each boy had gone alone, without his friends, do you think they all would have joined?

- In the evening, when the young men got home, they had "a lot of explaining to do." What do you think your parents would do if you enlisted in the armed forces during wartime without telling them first? What do you think their parents were thinking?

- How do you interpret the ending of this story? What happened to Will and the German who shared the foxhole?

- Of the four boys who went to war, whom do you think returned alive at the end of the war?

- What is the meaning of the picture at the end of the book?

- The posters and flyers pictured are quite forceful. Is this an example of propaganda? What separates propaganda from information or advertisement? Is it propaganda only if it is for the "other side?"

Activities:

- Many of the posters shown in this book promote enlisting and supporting the war effort. Some target those who remain at home—parents, shopkeepers, wives, and sweethearts. Have students examine their messages. Discuss the concepts of propaganda, recruitment, advertisement, and information related to these posters. Have students design their own posters or flyers to encourage young men and women to join the armed forces. You could use a current world conflict (e.g. the War in Iraq) and make the posters modern, or design World War I vintage-looking posters. For variety, students could pick different wars or conflicts and design posters to fit those eras.

- Research stories of similar events when soldiers reached across enemy lines in friendship, such as Jorgensen's *In Flander's Fields*.

Book Links: World War I

Granfield, Linda. *In Flander's Field: The story of the poem by John McCrae.* Illus. Janet Wilson. New York: Doubleday, 1995. (Grades 4-12)

Summary: Linda Granfield has put together a beautiful and informative book. She begins with the original poem, *In Flander's Field*, in John McCrae's handwriting, decorated by the illustrator. In subsequent pages, the author alternates between richly illustrated lines of the poem and pages of facts about World War I, the life of John McCrae, and the conditions on the battlefields where he worked as a battle surgeon. Either portion would stand alone, but they interweave to create a whole picture that leaves a lasting memory for the reader. For a similar picture book featuring John Magee, the Royal Canadian Air Pilot who wrote the famous poem "High Flight," see Granfield's *High Flight: A Story of World War II*.

Granfield, Linda. *Where Poppies Grow: A World War I Companion.* New York: Stoddart Publishing, 2001. (Grades 4-12)

Summary: While lengthy for a picture book, this forty-eight page nonfiction volume adds much to the discussion of World War I. Each two-page spread consists of a paragraph or two about a given topic, with various illustrations including photos of postcards, posters, photographs, and paintings. Each illustration is accompanied by a lengthy caption. The variety and quality of the illustrations give the reader the sense of being in a museum viewing the memorabilia first-hand. Each two-page spread will spark interest in a particular facet of the war effort. Assign a class project where students or small groups pick one topic to investigate further and produce a research report, poster, or PowerPoint presentation.

Jorgensen, Norman. *In Flander's Fields.* Illus. Brian Harrison-Lever. Vancouver, BC, Canada: Simply Read Books, 2003. (Grades 4-12)

Summary: In short, with poetic text and tinted line drawings, this book tells the old story of soldiers brought together on Christmas during World War I. In this version of the tale, the soldier goes out into the no-man's-land between the trenches to rescue a robin trapped in the barbed wire. The soldiers watch through their rifle sights as he frees the bird and returns to his trench. Many of these tales, including this one, end with the soldiers singing "Silent Night" together.

World War II—Concentration Camps and the Nazi Regime

McCann, Michelle Roehm. *Luba: The Angel of Bergen-Belsen*. Illus. Ann Marshall. Berkley, CA: Tricycle Press, 2003. (Grades 4-12)

Summary: Luba Tryszynska, who told her story to McCann for this book, was a Jewish prisoner in the Bergen-Belsen concentration camp. She lost her husband and child at Auschwitz, but remained alive because the Nazis thought she was a nurse. On her first night in Bergen-Belsen, she discovered 54 Dutch children in a field behind the camp. Soldiers had abandoned the children in the field rather than kill them, as ordered. Luba brought the children, some only infants, back to her barracks where the other women helped her hide the children. She found ways to steal and extort food, keeping 52 of the children alive until the end of the war. An epilogue details the fifty-year reunion celebrated by the surviving children, where Luba received the Dutch Silver Medal of Honor for Humanitarian Services. An explanation of the events of World War II and an extensive bibliography are included.

Discussion Questions:

- Imagine you were a soldier asked to take 54 children off into the woods and shoot them. What would happen to you if you disagreed or disobeyed? The dissenter was putting the other soldiers at risk—what choices did they have? What would your thoughts have been? Could you have killed the children and turned in the soldier who disobeyed? Could you face the consequences of choosing not to kill the children? How much better was it to leave them to freeze and starve to death?

- Luba and the other women chose to hide the children despite the real risk of discovery and death. What would you have done?

- The Nazis thought Luba was a nurse. Was she? Do we know?

- Would you be willing to lie and steal to save the children?

Activities:

- The bibliography included with this story lists several Web sites. Due to the subject matter, it is essential that you preview the sites for age appropriateness and suitability for your students. When you have selected sites that are appropriate, send students to those sites to investigate the concentration camps and look for answers to the questions raised in their minds by this book. Most of these Web sites will be useful with any of the books listed in this section.

- McCann's bibliography is an excellent example of the variety of sources one might use for a report or project. Use the bibliography as a tool to teach location and access of each kind of source as well as proper citation of unusual sources.

- Have students research the locations, numbers of people imprisoned, and years of operation of the concentration camps. Develop a large, poster-sized map of Europe with the information gathered.

Innocenti, Roberto and Christophe Gallaz. *Rose Blanche*. Illus. Roberto Innocenti. Mankato, Minnesota: Creative Education. 1985. (Grades 4-12)

Summary: Innocenti was a child when the Germans invaded his hometown in Italy. He has drawn on his memories and research to produce this striking book. Rose Blanche, a small girl in a German town, watches as the German soldiers arrive. Many townsmen become soldiers and leave, and the army trucks continue rolling through the village. When Rose sees a child try to escape from one of the army trucks, she follows the convoy out of town and discovers a concentration camp. She gives the hungry children what bread she has, and thereafter visits the camp daily, smuggling her own food to the children. When the German soldiers begin retreating as the allied troops advance, Rose goes once more to the camp, to discover it empty. Rose Blanche is last seen near the camp, surrounded by fog. She never returns to her family. The reader must infer what has happened. *Rose Blanche* takes its name from small group of young German citizens who protested the war.

Discussion Questions:

- This story is told in the first person for the first half of the story and then in the third person for the rest of the story. Why do you think the author made this switch?

- Roberto Innocenti has used a very unusual palette of colors in this book. What do you think was his purpose?

- What happened to Rose Blanche?

- Would a little girl have been able to visit a concentration camp without being caught by guards?

Activities:

There are a host of research projects suggested by this book. The best research projects come from questions students ask as they learn, and this book will elicit many questions. Here are some that may be worth investigating:

- The author states that he named the main character after a resistance group. Was there really a resistance group named Rose Blanche? How did they operate and what happened to them?

- Were there other protest or resistance groups in Germany and throughout Europe before and during the war? Find out their objectives, how they operated, and their successes and failures.

- Roberto Innocenti lived in Italy and saw the soldiers come to his town. Investigate what the war was like in different countries or cities. What part did Italy play in the war?

Kaplan, William, with Shelley Tanaka. *One More Border to Cross: The True Story of One Family's Escape From War-Torn Europe*. Illus. Stephen Taylor. Toronto, Ontario: Groundwood Books, 1998. (Grades 4-12)

Summary: The Kaplans were one of the last families given a visa by the Japanese Consul, Chinue Sugihara, before he left Lithuania. Sugihara wrote hundreds of visas against his country's orders. For more information, see *The Sugihara Story*, also referenced in this bibliography. William Kaplan tells the story of his father and grandparents' flight to Canada to begin a new life. He details the many difficulties and sacrifices made as the family travels by train through Russia and Asia, by boat to Japan and finally to Canada. Photographs, documents, and maps with extensive captions accompany illustrations of the family's journey. Of special interest is a reproduction of the actual visa, signed by Sugihara.

Discussion Questions:

■ The Kaplan family was very lucky, but it is also apparent that they were not poor. How did their financial resources help them along the way?

■ At several points in their journey, the Kaplans had to wait for permission to leave, for instance when the mother needed different permission to leave Lithuania because she was Russian. What would have happened to the family if at one of those critical points, things went wrong? How hard would it have been for Mother to catch up if she had not received permission at the last minute and rushed to get on the train as it was leaving?

■ The family had to leave most of their possessions behind in their hometown, then, as they traveled, more of their possessions were taken or given up as bribes. They started from scratch when they finally reached Canada, and began by working the land for one year despite their inexperience in farming. Why were they able to start over so successfully? What characteristics would a family need in order to survive and go on to thrive in their new home?

Activities:

■ Research possibilities are endless with this book. Ask students to find a portion that raises a question for them and research the question.

■ In the case of the Kaplans, the single most important document was the visa from Lithuania. In time, it became a historically significant document in the eyes of the entire world. Ask students to look within their own families for historical documents like the visa. While most families won't have such a stunning piece of history, many will have things such as an old homestead deed, immigration papers, discharge papers from military service, certificates or licenses (i.e. a teaching certificate, maritime captain's papers, marriage licenses) belonging to their ancestors. Sharing those and their significance to the family would be very interesting. With permission, make color copies for a display, accompanied by short student essays explaining the story behind each document. Students can also look in museums and on the Internet for copies of significant documents.

Mochizuki, Ken. *Passage to Freedom: The Sugihara Story*. Illus. Dom Lee. New York: Lee and Low, 1997. (Grades 4-12)

Summary: Mochizuki tells the true story of Chinue Sugihara, the Japanese consul in Lithuania in 1940. Forbidden by his government to write visas for Polish Jews who were seeking to escape the Nazis, he made the decision to write the visas anyway. He wrote hundreds of visas in the one-month period before Japan recalled him. It is estimated that Sugihara saved as many as ten thousand refugees. Written from the point of view of Chinue's son, Hiroki Sugihara, the text includes an afterword written by Hiroki. Sugihara and his family spent 18 months in a Soviet internment camp, and when they returned to Japan, he had to resign from the diplomatic corps. Dom Lee's muted, brown-toned paintings work well to help tell this story of having the courage to do what one believes is right despite the consequences. Used with *One More Border to Cross*, this will be even more powerful as the reader sees the risks taken by both the Sugihara family and families like the Kaplans.

Book Links: World War II— Concentration Camps and the Nazi Regime

Hoestlandt, Jo. *Star of Fear, Star of Hope*. Illus. Johanna Kang. New York: Walker, 1993. (Grades 4-12)

Summary: Young Helen is confused and angry when her best friend, Lydia, decides to go home during her birthday sleepover. The girls have heard Jews running from the Nazis, and Lydia is afraid for her Jewish family. Helen, who is not Jewish, does not understand the danger Lydia and her family face. To Helen's eternal regret, she says unkind words as Lydia leaves. In the morning, Helen's family finds that Lydia and her family have gone, never to be seen again. The illustrator has set this story in stark, yellow-toned pictures that compliment the text very well.

Bunting, Eve. *One Candle*. Illus. K. Wendy Popp. New York: HarperCollins, 2002. (Grades 4-12)

Summary: Grandmother and Great Aunt Rose use a potato and oil to make a candle to put in the window each Hanukkah. They tell the story of the Hanukkah candle they made from a stolen potato while imprisoned in Buchenwald concentration camp in Germany. This book gives the reader a picture of how difficult it is to maintain cultural or religious traditions in captivity, and how important those traditions become to those who are imprisoned.

Rubin, Susan Goldman. *Fireflies in The Dark: The Story of Friedl Dicker-Brandies and the Children of Terezin*. New York: Holiday House, 2000. (Grades 4-12)

Summary: Friedl Dicker-Brandies was an artist imprisoned in Terezin concentration camp. She worked there as a tutor of children. She taught drawing, and through art, gave hope to many children. Some of the children's drawings appear in this book. Unfortunately, neither Friedl nor most of the children she tutored survived the Holocaust. The author pieced the story together through research and contact with some of the children who did survive. While this is an unusual book because most picture books tell stories of survival, the message of hope is very strong. The story also serves as a reminder that, while there were many courageous acts, the reality was that most prisoners did not survive the death camps.

Polacco, Patricia. *The Butterfly*. New York: Philomel, 2000. (Grades 4-12)

Summary: Polacco's great aunt Marcel Solliliage hid Jews in her home during the Nazi Occupation of France. Marcel's daughter, Monique, awakens one night to find a "ghost" sitting in her room looking out the window. Later, she learns that the ghost is Sevrine, a girl her age whose family is hiding in the cellar of her home. This comes as a surprise, as Monique was unaware of her mother's clandestine activities. The girls become secret friends, and Monique tries to bring a little of the daytime world to Sevrine, including, once, a butterfly. When Marcel discovers the friendship, she and Monique move the family to the next safe house. Years later, Monique receives a message with a butterfly drawn on the page and the words "we live." The story is full of difficult discoveries, fearful moments, and very real peril. An author's note includes information about the real Marcel Solliliage and her activities in the war.

Adler, David. *Hiding from the Nazis*. Illus. Karen Ritz. New York: Holiday House, 1997. (Grades 4-12)

Summary: Adler tells the story of Lore Baer, born in Holland after her Jewish German parents had fled Germany. When the war came to Holland, Lore was hidden with a family in the countryside. Lore was only four when she left her family; she lived in hiding for several years. This book poignantly illustrates the feelings of young people reunited with families they barely remember.

Adler, David. *Hilde and Eli: Children of the Holocaust*. Illus. Karen Ritz. New York: Holiday House, 1994. (Grades 4-12)

Summary: From the first page of this account, the reader knows that both Hilde Rosenzweig and Eli Lax died in the Holocaust. While the two never met, Adler weaves their stories together masterfully. The prose in this book is clear, concise, and emotionless, leaving the reader to form his own conclusions. The effect is chilling at times as Adler reports very simply the facts of the children's deaths. An author's note explains how Adler got the information and what happened to the surviving siblings. The artist has used a muted palette to tell this story, adding touches of bright colors for emphasis. The illustrations are especially well suited to the starkness of the subject and text.

Adler, David. *Child of the Warsaw Ghetto*. Illus. Karen Ritz. New York: Holiday House, 1995. (Grades 4-12)

Summary: In 1939 in Poland, Nazi soldiers forced four hundred thousand Jews out of their homes into a seventy-three block area in Warsaw. Thousands died each month in the overcrowded ghetto. Eventually, those who survived the ghetto boarded trains to concentration camps. Froim Baum and his family lived in the ghetto, escaped to a nearby city, and were eventually captured by the Nazis and sent to Auschwitz. Froim narrowly escaped the gas chambers, but his mother and sisters did not. Of seven Baum children, only Froim and two brothers survived the war. Adler interviewed Froim (now called Erwin) Baum for this book.

Abells, Chana Byers. *The Children We Remember.* New York: Greenwillow, 1983. (Grades 4-12)

Summary: Simple, stark text accompanies photographs from the Archives of Yad Vashem, the Holocaust Martyrs' and Heroes' Remembrance Authority, in Jerusalem, Israel. Beginning with scenes from before the war, when children lived ordinary lives, the book shows the profound changes experienced by the Jewish people and the horrors visited upon the children by the Nazi Regime. The most unforgettable image shows a Nazi soldier about to shoot a child in a woman's arms, accompanied by the sentence "Sometimes they put children to death."

Feder, Paula Kurzband. *The Feather-Bed Journey.* Illus. Stacey Schuett. Morton Grove, Illinois: Albert Whitman, 1995. (Grades 4-8)

Summary: When her feather pillow rips and spills feathers, Grandma tells the story of the feather bed that she slept on as a child. From a Jewish ghetto in Poland during Nazi occupation, the little girl's bed travels with her to the countryside, where she lives in hiding with a Christian family. The girl's father and sisters died in the war. After the war, she is reunited with her mother and moves to America. Some years later, the farmer who had hidden her during the war sends a pillow made from the feather bed from her childhood.

Deedy, Carmen Agra. *The Yellow Star.* Illus. Henri Sorensen. Atlanta, Georgia: Peachtree, 2000. (Grades 4-8)

Summary: Told in poetic language, the legend of King Christian's courage against Nazi occupation is stirring. The Nazis required Jews to wear yellow stars to indicate that they were Jewish. The king himself, not a Jew, wears the star on his daily ride in the city, and suddenly every Dane is wearing the star. The author's note discusses the legend and shares facts uncovered in her research. She poses the questions: What if the king had worn the yellow star? What would happen today if we all stood together as a group to disallow injustice or violations of human rights? This is a thought-provoking story, and the author's questions will lead to a spirited discussion of Current World Problems in classes as well as units covering World War II.

Hughes, Shirley. *The Lion and the Unicorn.* New York: DK, 1999. (Grades 4-12)

Summary: This lengthy picture book tells the story of a Jewish boy, Lenny Levi, who is evacuated from London during World War II. His mother stays in London to work, and his father is fighting in the war. Among his few possessions are his father's medal, with pictures of a lion and a unicorn ready to fight. Lenny is sent to an old mansion in the country, complete with a walled garden. The estate reminds him of the story *The Secret Garden*. While exploring the grounds, he discovers a stone unicorn and meets a young, one-legged man home from the war. The focus of the story is learning to have courage in difficult situations. This book would be useful in a study of symbols in literature or literary allusion. The images of the lion and the unicorn as symbols could be explored. The allusion in the text to the book *The Secret Garden* might prompt discussion as well as extracurricular reading.

 # World War II—Japanese Internment

Mochizuki, Ken. *Baseball Saved Us*. Illus. Dom Lee. New York: Lee and Low, 1993. (Grades 4-12)

Summary: A Japanese American father builds a baseball field in an internment camp to give the residents hope and something to do during internment. His son learns to play baseball and is inspired to be better by the guard who watches them play. The skills and determination he learns in the camp help him when he returns home after the war and faces discrimination in school and on the baseball field. The book includes a brief explanation of internment camps and a discussion of the false perception of Japanese Americans as a threat to national security. *Baseball Saved Us* will be effective as a read-aloud in a history unit covering Japanese internment camps. It will pair nicely with *Snow Falling on Cedars* or *Farewell to Manzanar* in literature class as well.

Discussion Questions:

- *Baseball Saved Us* is told from the point of view of the child in the story. How would you tell the story from the father's point of view?

- What do you think the guard was thinking as he watched the prisoners build the field and then play baseball there?

- This boy was born in the United States. How would you feel if, even though you had been in the U.S. all your life, people suddenly considered you a possible enemy?

- What parallels can you see between the plight of the Japanese Americans in WWII and the Arab Americans in the present day war with Iraq? Would you characterize all Muslims or Arab Americans as potential terrorists or enemies of the U.S.? Defend your opinion.

Activities:

- Students could decide to research the Japanese American internment camps, choosing one close by their home, if possible.

- Compare/contrast the Japanese American camps with the Nazi camps of the same period—what were their aims, the reasons for their formation, the experiences the prisoners had? Who was imprisoned and how did the conditions differ? Were there other camps for Germans and/or Japanese in other countries?

- If reading the book in conjunction with *Snow Falling on Cedars* or *Farewell to Manzanar*, compare/contrast the experiences of the Japanese Americans in each of the camps. It would be interesting to learn more about the return of the Japanese Americans to their homes. Many lost possessions and land as well as suffered racist comments and actions.

Book Links: World War II—Japanese Internment

Uchida, Yoshiko. *The Bracelet.* Illus. Joanna Yardley. New York: Philomel Books, 1993. (Grades 4-8)

Summary: Emi and her mother and sister must move to a Japanese internment camp. Her friend Laurie gives her a bracelet to remember her by, but the bracelet is lost in the move to the camp. Emi is crushed, but eventually realizes that memory does not require a talisman. Her mother tells her that important things are never lost because we carry them "in our hearts and take with us no matter where we are sent." The author lived in a Japanese internment camp as a child.

Bunting, Eve. *So Far from the Sea.* Illus. Chris K. Soentpiet. New York: Clarion Books, 1998. (Grades 4-8)

Summary: Laura's family visits Manzanar War Relocation Camp in California for the last time before they move to Massachusetts. Laura's father lived there with his parents for three and one-half years. Manzanar was the first of the Japanese internment camps to be formed in 1942 and had a population of ten thousand people. It is now a National Historic Site. Bunting explores the feelings of the family toward the camp and the internment through the eyes of both Laura, who is visiting there, and her father, who lived there as a child.

Say, Allen. *Home of the Brave.* Boston: Houghton Mifflin, 2002. (Grades 4-12)

Summary: After a kayaking accident, a man enters a dreamlike state and visits an abandoned Japanese internment camp with two children. The children have nametags attached to their coats. When he peers inside an abandoned building, he discovers his own nametag there on the floor. Later, he finds his grandmother's nametag. This book has a spooky, otherworldly quality in both text and pictures and is well suited for a classroom discussion of the author/illustrator's interpretation and meaning.

 # World War II–Other Stories from the War

Tsuchiya, Yukio. *Faithful Elephants: A True Story of Animals, People and War.* Illus. Ted Lewin. New York: Houghton Mifflin, 1988. (Grades 4-12)

Summary: When Tokyo was bombed during World War II, the authorities feared that if the zoo were destroyed, the wild animals would wreak havoc in the city. It fell to the zookeepers to carry out the decision to kill all the animals, but the elephants posed a problem. The huge animals seemed to sense their food was poisoned, and syringes broke before penetrating their skin. The only solution was to starve the elephants to death, an excruciating experience for both the animals and the people. In the scope of World War II, this book presents is a small incident, but it serves to remind and educate readers about the real costs of war. In the introduction to the book, journalist Cheiko Akiyama recounts how he has read this story aloud in many of his lectures throughout the world. He says, "My act of reading this story seems trivial, however…strongholds of peace have been built in the hearts of adults and children when they realize the sorrow, misery, horror and foolishness of war." The simple act of reading this book aloud as part of a World War II unit will hook the students into the realities of war in a powerful, emotional way.

Discussion Questions:

- What would you have done if you were the elephant trainer?

- Why did the other zookeepers ignore it when the trainer fed and watered the animals?

- Imagine you lived near the zoo. How would you feel about a decision made to kill the animals to protect your safety?

Activities:

- Have students write a persuasive essay detailing why the zookeepers should or should not euthanize the animals at the zoo. Research for supporting details could include the specific dangers posed by the animals if they were loose in the bombed city, methods of calming animals in that case, options for relocating the animals to safer places, and alternative methods of euthanizing animals.

- Stage a debate between students taking positions for and against euthanizing the animal. Allow time before the debate for research to find supporting facts. In a Current World Problems class, place the debate in the context of the present day and a similar threat to a major city in the United States.

Marx, Trish. *Hanna's Cold Winter.* Illus. Barbara Knutson. Minneapolis, Minnesota: Carolrhoda Books, 1993. ((Grades 4-8)

Summary: Marx tells the true story of the Budapest zoo, famous for its hippos, especially Hanna, a great favorite. During World War II, winters were unusually cold, and food was very hard to find. The people of Budapest kept their beloved hippos alive by donating their straw floor mats, hats, and slippers to feed them. *Hanna's Cold Winter* makes a good contrast to *The Faithful Elephants*. What prompted two cities to make such different decisions about the zoo?

Lee, Emily. *Nim and the War Effort.* Illus. Yangsook Choi. New York: Farrar, Straus, and Giroux, 1997. (Grades 4-8)

Summary: Nim's school is holding a paper drive to help the war effort. Nim is determined to win the contest to see who can bring in the most newspapers. The biggest boy in school plans to win at any cost, even by stealing papers from the paper vendor. Nim's time is limited because she attends Chinese school every day after school, but she finds a clever and courageous way to win the contest. Nim's relationship with her Grandfather and the personal consequences of her actions give the reader a glimpse into San Francisco's Chinatown in the 1940s. This book works well as a lead-in to a discussion about the home front war effort in the United States— who was involved, what was recycled or rationed, what sacrifices were made at home, how people's lives changed. Students can compare and contrast the WWII war effort and conditions at home with those of the Vietnam War, the Gulf War, or the War in Iraq.

Hunter, Sara Hoagland. *The Unbreakable Code*. Illus. Julia Miner. Flagstaff, AZ: Northland Publishing, 1996. (Grades 4-12)

Summary: John, a young Navajo boy, is reluctant to move away from the reservation. As Grandfather helps him deal with the fear of leaving, he tells John about his role as a code talker in World War II. The author interviewed many code talkers to get the information for this story. There were 420 code talkers in all, and they saved countless lives in the Pacific using the unbreakable code based on the Navajo language. An appendix includes the original code for the 26 letters of the alphabet and a sample of coded words.

Raven, Margot Theis. *Mercedes and the Chocolate Pilot: A True Story of the Berlin Airlift and the Candy that Dropped from the Sky.* Illus. Gijsbert van Frankenbuyzen. Chelsea, MI: Sleeping Bear Press, 2002. (Grades 4-8)

Summary: Three years after World War II ended, the Berlin Airlift provided food to the people of West Berlin. From 1948 until 1949, they delivered more than 2.3 million tons of supplies. One of the pilots, Gail S. Halvorsen, began making handkerchief parachutes loaded with candy, and dropping them as he made his supply runs. With the help of volunteers in the United States, Halvorsen and his squadron dropped more than 250,000 little candy "bombs" on Berlin in the fifteen months of the Airlift. This book tells the true story of the candy drops and the correspondence between Halvorsen and a little girl, Mercedes Simon.

 ## Civil Rights for All

Hamanaka, Sheila. *The Journey: Japanese Americans, Racism, and Renewal.* New York: Orchard Books, 1990. (Grades 4-12)

Summary: Sheila Hamanaka painted a five-panel mural about Japanese American history, partly as "a personal inquiry focusing on events that changed my family's life." For *The Journey,* she selected scenes from the mural and added a combination of picture captions and text boxes describing what each segment represents. The mural begins with the early twentieth century when Japanese Americans labored in the farm and fisheries industries and continues on to the present day struggle for reparations to those interred in World War II. Hamanaka includes scenes of Japanese internment during World War II, demonstrations against internment camps for Communists proposed in the 1950s, and anti-war protests in the Vietnam era.

Activities:

- Study historical murals to see how they portray historical events. Compare and contrast different styles of murals.

- Hamanaka mentions that the government secretly built new camps under Title II of the International Security Act of 1950, called the Emergency Detention Act. While the camps never opened, the intent was to detain people who disagreed with the government. Senator Joseph R. McCarthy was leading investigations into "Communists" at that time. Find out more about the link between the McCarthy hearings in Congress and the Emergency Detention Act. The Act remained in effect until 1971. Research how it functioned for those 20 years and how and why it was enacted and repealed. Compare the Emergency Detention Act with current laws such as the Homeland Security Act and the Patriot Act.

- Compare the facts given here about Japanese internment camps with the versions in other picture books. Are there major differences in people's experiences? What were the similarities? Do the fictional accounts contradict one another? How can you decide which version is accurate?

Yin. *Coolies*. Illus. Chris Soentpiet. New York: Philomel, 2001. (Grades 4-12)

Summary: Grandmother tells a young boy the story of his great-great-great grandfather and his brother, who came to America to help build the Transcontinental Railroad. The brothers fled China to find work and sent money home to support their families. This book illustrates the difficult life and poor working conditions of the Chinese laborers on the railroad. Chinese laborers, called coolies by the overseers, were considered the lowest of all workers, and consequently, were assigned the hardest jobs for the least pay. The Chinese workers strike when they discover Irish laborers earn more for the same work, but the strike is unsuccessful. The overseers starve the Chinese laborers until they give in, worried more about their families back home than their own plight. The two brothers support each other, succeed despite the conditions, and eventually, earn enough money to bring their families to America

Discussion Questions:

- When the Chinese workers discover they earn less than other laborers, they believe it is because of their race. What do you think? Irish immigrants worked the railroad, too. Were the Irish better than the Chinese? Were the Irish paid as much as non-immigrant workers? Why do you think there was such a difference in pay rates?

- Why do you think the workers gave up their strike? What would you have done in their situation?

Activities:

- Research the building of the Transcontinental Railroad. Where did all the workers come from? What was the pay scale? How many workers died during the building of the railroad? What was important about making the railroad transcontinental?

- The issue of unequal pay for equal work still exists in present day work forces. Students can find examples from around the world to research and discuss. Outsourcing of United States jobs to lower paid foreign workers is a current political topic and brings up some of the same issues. Researching these subjects will lead students to impassioned discussions or debate.

Book Links: Civil Rights for All

Littlesugar, Amy. *Freedom School, Yes!* Illus. Floyd Cooper. New York: Philomel, 2001. (Grades 4-8)

Summary: In 1964, the Mississippi Summer Project involved more than six hundred volunteers from all over the United States in an effort to help African Americans in Mississippi gain their civil rights. Among the volunteers were men and women who became Freedom School teachers. In this story, a black family hosts a Freedom School Teacher in their home while she is teaching the children of the community. The Freedom School is unpopular with the racist portions of the local population, and the family and the school are in real danger. *Freedom School* gives readers an example of courage in the face of hatred and of the civil rights movement in action.

Ray, Mary Lyn. *Basket Moon.* Illus. Barbara Cooney. New York: Little Brown, 1999. (Grades 4-8)

Summary: This book illustrates prejudice in a different situation. A young boy grows up in the countryside, learning from his family and community how to make beautiful "Bushwhacker" baskets, which his Pa takes to town to sell. The revenue from the baskets provides the income for the family, and the sturdy, beautiful baskets are highly prized. When the boy is old enough to accompany his father to town, he experiences the prejudice of the townspeople toward the "bushwhacker hillbillies." He struggles to come to terms with the attitudes of the townsfolk and with his own conflicted feelings about the baskets and his life in the country. Barbara Cooney's pictures reflect the folk art of the period and complement the text.

 ## Other Times, Other Places

Lawrence, Jacob. *The Great Migration.* New York: HarperCollins, 1993. (Grades 4-12)

Summary: In 1941-42, Jacob Lawrence painted a series of 60 paintings depicting the journey of African Americans who migrated from the rural South to find jobs in the industrial cities of the North. This migration happened around the time of World War I, when many workers from northern factories had gone to fight in the war. Lawrence's family migrated from South Carolina to New Jersey, where he was born. His mother moved the family to New York City when he was thirteen. The forward explains his research and the methods he used to create these paintings. The text describes the migration simply, almost starkly, effectively melding with the paintings. The text is followed by a poem entitled "Migration," written by Walter Dean Myers.

Discussion Questions:

- Imagine painting 60 paintings all at once within a year. Mr. Lawrence describes how he painted them; spread out on sawhorse and board tables, mixing the colors one by one, so the paintings would share the same palette. How would you keep the paintings organized during the process? Do you think he sketched out each painting first?

- What would it be like to try to tell a story in a series of images? What does this make you curious about?

Activities:

- Research Jacob Lawrence. In the forward to the book, Lawrence states that he had to paint things he had not painted before: interiors, scenes of violence, and rural landscapes. Look at the paintings he did before 1941 to compare and contrast his styles and subjects. After he finished these paintings, what kind of pictures did he paint in the years that followed? Was there a lasting influence on his subject matter or style? How do you know this?

- Have students write migration poems of their own based on one or more of the paintings in the book, or find a different painting to use as a prompt for poems.

Book Links: Other Times, Other Places

Fitzpatrick Marie-Louise. *The Long March*. Hillsboro, OR: Beyond Words, 1998. (Grades 4-12)

Summary: In 1847, the Oklahoma Choctaws collected and sent $170, a huge sum in those days, to Ireland to help the Irish people during the Great Famine. Choona, a Choctaw teenager, tells the story. During the discussion about helping the Irish, Choona hears, for the first time, the story of the Long March of the Choctaw from their ancestral home in Mississippi to Oklahoma, where he was born. This is a moving coming of age story as well as the story of the Choctaw nation and the Irish Famine. Irish writer/ illustrator Marie-Louise Fitzpatrick and Choctaw editor Gary Whitedeer collaborated on this book. Whitedeer is the director of Celts and American Indians Together (CAIT), a bi-national organization of Irish and American Indians formed to raise $1.7 million for famine relief, thus, "completing the circle of giving begun 150 years ago by the Choctaw." Additional information is included at the end of the narrative.

Bunting, Eve. *Train to Somewhere*. Illus. Ronald Himler. New York: Clarion Books, 1996. (Grades 4-8)

Summary: Trains called Orphan Trains existed from the 1850s until the 1920s, transporting approximately one hundred thousand homeless children to homes in the Midwest. Many children were in fact orphans, others simply abandoned at orphanages by parents who could not care for them. The Children's Aid Society tried to place the children with loving families, although the results were not always happy. Bunting tells a fictional tale of fourteen children sent from New York City on a train to small towns in the Midwest, hoping to find homes with people who met the train wanting to adopt children. This story explores the feelings of some of those children as they journeyed toward an unknown new life.

For more information on the Orphan Trains in a slightly longer format:

Warren, Andrea. *Orphan Train Rider: One Boy's True Story*. Boston, MA: Houghton Mifflin, 1996. (Grades 4-12)

Littlefield, Holly. *Children of the Orphan Trains*. Minneapolis, MN: Carolrhoda, 2001. (Grades 4-12)

Lamb, Nancy, and Children of Oklahoma City. *One April Morning*. Illus. Floyd Cooper. New York: Lothrop, Lee and Shepard, 1996. (Grades 4-12)

Summary: The April 1995 bombing of the Federal Building in Oklahoma City touched lives all over the country and the world. For this moving book, the author had conversations with children all over Oklahoma City about the bombing, its aftermath, and the grieving and healing process. The children are credited and quoted in the book. This is a thoughtful, thought-provoking book written in a gentle, yet very open way, about the feelings and perceptions of the children.

Shea, Pegi Deitz. *The Whispering Cloth*. Illus. Anita Riggo and You Yang. Honesdale, Pennsylvania: Boyds Mills Press, 1995. (Grades 4-12)

Summary: The Ban Vinai refugee camp near Chiang Khan, Thailand housed Hmong refugees from Laos from 1976 to 1995. The author of this book visited the Ban Vinai refugee camp and watched Hmong women stitching tapestries to sell in the "Widow's Store" in the camp. A young girl she met there became the model for Mai, the main character in this story. In *The Whispering Cloth*, Mai, who lives in the camp with her grandmother, learns to design and embroider the pa'ndau, a traditional tapestry of the Hmong. She learns technique along with the necessity of telling a story with the cloth. She believes she has no story to tell, but learns that perhaps she does—the story of her life and future. The embroidery shown in the book is crafted by You Yang, who spent seventeen years living in the refugee camps before coming to America.

Wallace, Ian. *Boy of the Deeps*. New York: DK Publishing, 1999. ((Grades 4-8)

Summary: Ian Wallace tells the story of his own grandfather who worked in the mines in England. I serves as a universal story of a young man who goes into the mines to begin a lifetime of working coal. For the purposes of the story, Wallace chose as his setting Cape Breton, Nova Scotia, at the turn of the century. He tells of the first day Jamie goes down into the mine to work with his father. On that first day, Jamie and his father are trapped by a cave-in and must work to meet the rescuers halfway. This book clearly shows the dangers of the mines at that time and beyond. It also illustrates the pride the men had in mining.

Lasky, Kathryn. *Marven of the Great North Woods.* Illus. Kevin Hawkes. New York: Harcourt Brace, 1997. (Grades 4-12)

Summary: Ten-year-old Marven is sent away from the city during the influenza epidemic of 1918. He spends the winter in a logging camp, making friends with the French-Canadian loggers who work and live there. One of the interesting points of discussion is why Marven was chosen to go away rather than his sisters. The author explains this in the author's note, but students will wonder as the story progresses. This is a true story. The author's father is Marven.

Myers, Walter Dean. *Patrol: An American Soldier in Vietnam.* Illus. Ann Grifalconi. New York: HaperCollins, 2002. (Grades 7-12)

Summary: *Patrol* is a poetic story of one day in the life of a young soldier on patrol in 1960s Vietnam. It is chilling in its portrayal of a young man's fears and the reality of being a soldier. The young American soldier comes face-to-face with his enemy and clearly articulates his mixed feelings in that situation. The two soldiers each wait for the other to shoot, both obviously feeling the same fears. Before either soldier can fire, the American troops pull out. The sense of relief is immense. This is a powerful story.

Marx, Trish. *One Boy from Kosovo.* Photographs Cindy Karp. New York: HarperCollins, 2000. (Grades 4-12)

Summary: In the process of documenting one family's experience in the Brazda refugee camp in Macedonia, the author and illustrator give a clear picture of the causes and effects of the ethnic cleansing policy in Kosovo in the 1990s. Edi and his family flee Kosovo to the camp in Macedonia to avoid the Serbian soldiers and the atrocities committed in Kosovo. When Edi and his family were in the camp, 30,000 people were housed there. The book chronicles the family's flight to the camp and their life there.

Millard, Dr. Anne. *A Street Through Time: A 12,000-Year Walk Through History.* Illus. Steve Noon. New York: DK, 1998. (Grades 4-12)

Summary: This oversized book chronicles the history of one street beside a European river, beginning in 10,000 B.C. and continuing through the ages to the present day. Each two-page spread includes a short paragraph setting the stage for that era. The detailed picture of the street allows the reader to view the daily lives of the residents and the changes in the buildings and landscape. Some of the buildings in each picture are cutaway to show the interior. Individual pictures are labeled for clarity and each panorama is bordered by extra facts. A fictional time traveler hides on each page, and presents a quiz and glossary at the end of the book.

Chapter $\boxed{5}$

Picture Book

Biographies

Picture book biographies have become very popular in recent years. A picture book biography, often telling, in a short format, the basic facts about a famous person, is a solid beginning when looking for information about a that person, In general, there is as much as or more information in a picture book biography than teachers would expect from a student report, arranged in a much more pleasing format than an encyclopedia article. While there may not be time to go into the lives of all the players in a particular era, by taking time to read aloud a short biography, the teacher can communicate much information about a person who was part of the larger time period. This gives the student a more down-to-earth look at the era, illustrating the conditions and assumptions that the people worked under at that time in history. Some biographies focus on a pivotal event in a famous person's life. Narrowing the breadth of the subject allows the biographer to increase the depth of the story. Picture book biographies also generate plenty of questions for further research into both the person's life and actions and the events of the time.

Students often ask librarians for an additional book about a famous person, rejecting the picture book biography as not having enough information. The student who asks for another book because "this one doesn't tell when and where this person was born and died" has probably overlooked this information. While picture book biographers must choose facts carefully and be selective in their choices, students have seldom accessed all the information contained within the source before deciding that they need more information. Librarians and teachers must stress comprehension and note taking when reading picture book biographies in order to avoid this trap. Students need to remember to think about their questions before reading so when they come to a useful piece of information, they will take note of it at that time. Finally, most picture biographies provide the sheer pleasure of reading fascinating stories of people's lives.

All of the featured authors and illustrators exhibit high levels of scholarship and have researched their subjects thoroughly, often traveling to ruins, museums, and libraries in the country or area where their subject worked and lived. Most include bibliographies of sources and suggest books for further reading. The biographies that follow are grouped alphabetically by author.

Andronik, Catherine M. *Hatshepsut: His Majesty, Herself.* Illus. Joseph Daniel Fiedler. New York: Atheneum, 2001. (Grades 4-12)

Summary: Hatshepsut was the wife of Pharaoh Tuthmosis II. When he died, she became regent for his infant son, as was the custom. Over seven years, her regency became more and more powerful until she finally had herself crowned pharaoh. She ruled as king for twenty-two years, until her death. This biography includes a timeline and a thorough story of Hatshepsut's reign as Pharaoh of Egypt. The author includes the known facts, the theories, and a discussion of the reasons for the difficulty of researching the life of Egypt's only successful woman Pharaoh.

Bedard, Michael. *Emily.* Illus. Barbara Cooney. New York: Doubleday, 1992. (Grades 4-8)

Summary: Emily Dickinson lived a life of self-chosen isolation. She never left the property she shared with her sister and was seldom seen by anyone. The fictional little girl who lives next door calls her the Myth, and is very curious about Emily. One day, the girl's mother takes her along when she goes to play the piano for Emily. The mother plays in the parlor, but Emily is too ill to come downstairs, so, she listens from upstairs. The little girl sneaks up the stairs to have a conversation with The Myth. Read this book aloud when studying Dickinson's poetry, for a glimpse into her character.

Brown, Don. *Far Beyond the Garden Gate: Alexandra David-Neel's Journey to Lhasa.* Boston: Houghton Mifflin, 2002. (Grades 4-12)

Summary: Alexandra David-Neel, who was the most famous woman in France in her time, became a scholar of Buddhism and Tibet in the early 1900s. She was in her mid-fifties in 1924 when she trekked thousands of miles to reach Lhasa, the Tibetan capital. The fact that David-Neel was the first Western woman to enter Lhasa makes her story even more amazing. Don Brown has also written and illustrated several other picture book biographies of exceptional women.

Book Links: Don Brown

Brown, Don. *Ruth Law Thrills a Nation.* New York: Ticknor & Fields, 1993. (Grades 4-12)

Brown, Don. *Alice Ramsey's Grand Adventure.* Boston: Houghton Mifflin, 1997. (Grades 4-12)

Brown, Don. *A Voice from the Wilderness: the Story of Anna Howard Shaw.* Boston: Houghton Mifflin, 2001. (Grades 4-12)

Brown, Don. *Uncommon Traveler: Mary Kingsley in Africa.* Boston: Houghton Mifflin, 2000. (Grades 4-12)

Burleigh, Robert. *Black Whiteness: Admiral Byrd Alone in the Antarctic.* Illus. Walter Lyon Krudop. New York: Atheneum, 1998. (Grades 4-12)

Summary: Admiral Byrd spent almost six months alone on the continent of Antarctica in 1934. Robert Burleigh uses poetic language to describe this adventure, interspersing journal entries in Byrd's voice with a narrative telling the sequence and facts of the stay. While not a biography of Byrd's life and accomplishments, this slice of his life and adventures will spark interest in finding out more about the explorer and the conditions that explorers and scientists faced in this time in history.

Discussion Questions:

- Why did Byrd turn off the heat at night? What happened when the gas in the ice cave affected him?

- Why did Byrd decide not to tell the base camp crew that he was ill? Do you think the people at Little America suspected that he was not well? What clues alerted the radio crew to his illness?

Activities:

- *Black Whiteness* is an excellent book to use as a "think-aloud." When reading the book aloud, stop to model for students the kind of thinking that good readers do as they read. Talk to the students about the questions the text raises in their minds, comment on a specific piece of text that is especially moving, relate the ideas in the text to your own experiences, predict what might happen next, or stop to puzzle out the meaning of a word or phrase.

- Using excerpts from the poetic language in the book, discuss the author's purpose in his word choice. Use a phrase such as "afternoon skies that shatter like 'broken goblets' as tiny ice crystals fall across the face of the sun." Here, Burleigh has quoted Byrd, and then, added his own words to create an unforgettable image in the reader's mind. Discuss the role of the illustrator in making the pictures reflect the elegance of the text.

- Research the life of Admiral Richard Byrd. What were his major accomplishments? How did this episode fit into his life? What kind of reputation did he have among other explorers and scientists?

- Research the exploration and scientific studies done in the Antarctic. Compare and contrast the life of field scientists today with conditions in Byrd's time. The continent's conditions have not changed. What has technology done for us in making the continent more accessible? How do our scientists cope today, and what conditions are still limiting to research? Investigate the case of Dr. Jerri Nielsen, a doctor who had to treat herself for breast cancer while at a scientific station at the South Pole. The incident was widely reported in newspapers and periodicals, and she wrote about her experience in the book *Icebound*. Students could choose to read *Icebound* for an extra credit report or as part of a larger study of conditions in Antarctica. (*Icebound* is an adult book, and not suggested below high school level.)

Book Links: Robert Burleigh

Burleigh, Robert. *Who Said That?: Famous Americans Speak*. Illus. David Catrow. New York: Henry Holt, 1997. (Grades 4-12)

Summary: David Catrow's irreverent illustrations make this book especially fun for use in middle school. The satirical nature of the illustrations will appeal to many kids, and librarians and teachers will find this book useful in a discussion of satire and caricature. Along with quotations from many important figures from the last two centuries, the author includes a bit of information on each person.

Burleigh, Robert. *Flight: The Journey of Charles Lindbergh*. Illus. Mike Wimmer. New York: Philomel Books, 1991. (Grades 4-12)

Burleigh, Robert. *Home Run: The Story of Babe Ruth*. Illus. Mike Wimmer. San Diego, CA: Silver Whistle, 1998. (Grades 4-12)

Christensen, Bonnie. *The Daring Nellie Bly: America's Star Reporter*. New York: Knopf, 2003. (Grades 4-12)

Summary: Nellie Bly was a reporter and adventuress in 1864, in an era when women's career choices were extremely limited. She fought against those limits all her life, becoming a daredevil newspaper reporter. Her two most notorious stunts are among those chronicled in this book. First, she committed herself to an insane asylum to research a news story exposing the horrible treatment of women in that facility. Bly's second and most famous adventure was a challenge to the concept outlined in the Jules Verne novel *Around the World in 80 Days*. She successfully traveled around the world alone in less than 80 days. The illustrations reflect the style appropriate to the newspapers of the era.

Cooney, Barbara. *Eleanor*. New York: Viking, 1996. (Grades 4-8)

Summary: Eleanor Roosevelt's childhood was privileged but lonely and unpleasant. Her family considered her ugly and dull, and frequently reminded her of their disappointment. Her mother died when she was eight, so, Eleanor grew up in the household of her Grandmother Hall. When Eleanor was 15, Grandmother shipped her to England to boarding school. At school, she blossomed under the attention of the headmistress, learning the skills and deportment that helped her in her adult life. Eleanor's accomplishments as First Lady and humanitarian are noted at the end of the narrative.

Demi. *Muhammad*. New York: Margaret K. McElderry Books, 2003. (Grades 4-12)

Summary: Demi tells the story of the life of Muhammad, the Prophet who founded Islam. This biography begins with Muhammad's childhood, continuing on to his revelations from the angel Gabriel, which began at age forty and continued for twenty-three years. The revelations, recorded by Muhammad's scribes, make up the text of the Koran. This biography is simply written and shows great respect and reverence for the subject. Demi has followed Islamic tradition in not picturing Muhammad or his family, using a golden, featureless figure instead. Her beautifully detailed illustrations are a major part of the appeal of this book, but equal attention to detail and authenticity is evident in both text and illustrations.

Discussion Questions:

- Muhammad granted religious tolerance to Christians and Jewish people who paid a tax. How does that differ from world leaders in other areas over the centuries? Compare the life the Pilgrims sought to escape when leaving England to the life they might have had under Muhammad's rule.

- Muhammad received a varied education due in part to the deaths in his family. How do you think his various living experiences contributed to his view of the world?

Activities:

- On the back cover, a scholarly reviewer writes, "Demi attempts to remove prevailing misconceptions about Islam and Muhammad and to provide correct historical information in a beautiful manner." Investigate the current and prevailing misconceptions about Islam, especially in light of the events of September 11, and try to discover what differences there are in the Islamic world today in the interpretation of the Koran.

- Using one of Demi's books, study the art techniques she uses to produce such rich and stunning illustrations.

Book Links: Demi

Demi. *The Dalai Lama: A Biography of the Tibetan Spiritual and Political Leader*. New York: Henry Holt, 1998. (Grades 4-12)

Demi. *Gandhi*. New York: Margaret K. McElderry Books, 2001. (Grades 4-12)

Demi. *Buddha*. New York: Henry Holt, 1996. (Grades 4-12)

Dinetti, Michelle. *Painting the Wind*. Illus. Kevin Hawkes. New York: Little, Brown, 1996. (Grades 4-12)

Summary: Dinetti imagines a story featuring Vincent Van Gogh's charwoman and her daughter, based on a fragment from a letter Van Gogh wrote to his brother. The daughter admires the work of the artist, but the townspeople fear "Fou Roux" the crazy painter and eventually get the mayor to ban him from living in the town. The charwoman's little girl finds the courage to go to Van Gogh's house before he leaves to tell him how much she appreciates his painting. See *The Yellow House: Vincent* *van Gogh and Paul Gauguin Side by Side* by Susan Goldman Rubin for another vignette from the life of Van Gogh.

Fradin, Dennis Brindell. *Nicolaus Copernicus: The Earth is a Planet.* Illus. Cynthia Von Buhler. New York: Mondo, 2003. (Grades 4-12)

Summary: In the 1500s, scholars believed that the earth was the center of the universe and the sun, moon, stars, and planets revolved around it. This biography tells the story of Nicolaus Copernicus, a priest and physician in Poland, who spent his lifetime studying the stars. He came to agree with the ancient Greek astronomer Aristarchus, who believed that the earth and planets orbit around the sun. Just before his death, Copernicus published his book, *Concerning the Revolutions of the Heavenly Spheres.* His theory was controversial, but proven by Galileo Galilei and Isaac Newton nearly a century later.

Grimes, Nikki. *Talkin' about Bessie: The Story of Aviator Elizabeth Coleman.* Illus. Lewis, E. B. New York: Scholastic, 2002. (Grades 4-12)

Summary: In her book, Grimes uses the device of different people "talkin' about Bessie" in a gathering after her funeral to present the life of Bessie Coleman. Coleman was born in 1892 and was only eleven years old when the Wright brothers took their historic flight. No one would teach a black woman to fly in the United States in the 1890s, so Coleman trained in France and became the first black woman aviator. She did daredevil stunts at many air shows and dreamed of starting a flying school for blacks in the United States. Each person who speaks, from her parents and siblings to friends, associates, fans, and journalists, shares his or her impressions of Bessie in the form of poetry.

Harness, Cheryl. *The Revolutionary John Adams.* Washington D. C.: National Geographic, 2003. (Grades 4-12)

Summary: Cheryl Harness puts a great deal of information into the picture book format. The narrative tells the story of John Adams's life, from birth until death. The writing style allows you to get a glimpse of the personality as well as the accomplishments of the Revolutionary leader and second President of the United States. Harness shows Adams's fierce loyalty to the United States as well as a deep love and commitment to his wife, Abigail, and his family. The text is augmented with pictures that include tidbits of information, maps, heavily annotated timelines, and quotes from letters Adams wrote and received in correspondence with Abigail, Thomas Jefferson and others. Packed with well-researched information, this book will be useful in any study of early American history.

Discussion Questions:

- John Adams chose to defend the King's soldiers accused in the Boston Massacre when five Americans were killed. It was an unpopular decision, especially since he was on the political side of the American Revolutionaries. Why do you think he made that decision?

- Abigail Adams wrote to her husband on March 31, 1776 that in making a new code of laws, the Continental Congress should "remember the ladies." What do you think she meant?

- In John Adams's time, the rules of presidential elections were different than today. The candidate who won became President, and the loser became the Vice President. John Adams ran against Thomas Jefferson and won, so, Jefferson became Adams's Vice President. Would it be hard to be the Vice President for someone you worked to defeat in an election? Do you think that contributed to the bad feelings between Adams and Jefferson? Do you think that method of election was changed because of possible problems with rivals becoming partners after the election?

Activities:

- Harness's books contain excellent examples of reports that are not the standard ten-page research paper. Many facts appear in pleasing, poster-like maps and timelines. In one illustration, Adams stands on a stage, with curtains pulled back revealing a map of the United States and an illustrated timeline listing many important world events in his time. Students could design a poster as a report, showing evidence of much research in the process of finding the right facts to put on their poster.

- Cheryl Harness's Website, <http://www.cherylharness.com/> is worth visiting for more information on her books and curriculum ideas for grades kindergarten through grade 6. Harness also recommends the "This Day in History" portion of History Net, <http://www.historynet.com/tih/tih0111/>.

- Students could choose one of Harness's books for a book report. A report on a nonfiction book would need to include facts learned from the text, a basic story of the person's life and his/her significance to history, rather than the elements of fiction such as plot and characters.

- This book touches on many aspects of the Revolutionary War. Have students pick a topic for additional research. Possibilities include the Stamp Act, the tenure of John Adams as President, the Boston Tea Party, and many others. Students could plan an oral presentation of the results of their research. Presentation ideas include a poster or map, a skit, or a PowerPoint slide show.

Book Links: Cheryl Harness

Harness, Cheryl. *Ghosts of the White House*. New York: Simon and Schuster, 1998. (Grades 4-8)

Summary: *Ghosts of the White House* may appeal to a younger audience, given that the vehicle is the fictional story of young Sara, who meets the ghosts of former presidents. Each president gives Sara his perspective on the job and the times. The information, however, is solid, and shows the way the different residents of the White House reflected their times and influenced the United States.

Harness, Cheryl. *Abe Lincoln Goes to Washington: 1837-1865*. Washington D. C.: National Geographic Society, 1996. (Grades 4-12)

Summary: This biography focuses on Abraham Lincoln as he became a lawyer, married Mary Todd, became a senator, and eventually, was elected President of the

United States. The author successfully gives the reader a full picture of Lincoln in all facets of his life, the good times, and the bad. The Gettysburg Address is printed; along with the fact that Lincoln and many others thought the speech was a "wet blanket" at the time. There are many opportunities here for questions from students that can lead to further research into the life of Lincoln and the facts of the Civil War.

Harness, Cheryl. *Young Abe Lincoln.* Washington D. C.: National Geographic, 1996. (Grades 4-8)

Harness, Cheryl. *Young John Quincy.* Washington D. C.: National Geographic, 1994. (Grades 4-8)

Harness, Cheryl. *Young Teddy Roosevelt.* Washington D. C.: National Geographic, 1998. (Grades 4-7)

Harness, Cheryl. *George Washington.* Washington, D. C.: National Geographic, 2000. (Grades 4-7)

Harness, Cheryl. *Ghosts of the Civil War.* New York: Simon and Schuster, 2002. (Grades 4-12)

Harness, Cheryl. *Ghosts of the Twentieth Century.* New York: Simon and Schuster, 2000. (Grades 4-12)

Harness, Cheryl. *Rabble Rousers: 20 Women Who Made a Difference.* New York: Dutton, 2003. (Grades 4-12)

Harness, Cheryl. *Remember the Ladies.* New York: HarperCollins, 2001. (Grades 4-12)

Lasky, Kathryn. *A Voice of Her Own: The Story of Phillis Wheatley, Slave Poet.* Illus. Paul Lee. Cambridge, MA: Candlewick Press, 2003. (Grades 4-12)

Summary: Phillis Wheatley was a girl of about seven when she was brought from Africa to Boston and sold to the Wheatley family as a household slave. Mrs. Wheatley taught her to read and write as a sort of experiment, even though it was against local tradition in New England to educate slaves. Phillis became a poet, and through the determination of Mrs. Wheatley, a book of her poetry was published in England. The Wheatleys freed Phillis about the same time that her poems were published. Use this story when studying slavery as it existed in the northern United States, as practices were somewhat different from the Southern states. This book is also a wonderful example of the value of education in helping people develop a voice of their own.

Lasky, Kathryn. *Born in the Breezes: The Seafaring Life of Joshua Slocum.* Illus. Walter Lyon Krudop. New York: Orchard Books, 2001. (Grades 4-12)

Summary: Short, illustrated chapters tell the life story of Joshua Slocum, one of the greatest sea captains of the nineteenth century and the first person to circumnavigate the globe alone. Slocum's life and accomplishments rival those of many of the explorers of the time, but he is less famous. Add this book to a unit on explorers to broaden the knowledge of students beyond the standard explorers featured in history textbooks.

Book Links: Kathryn Lansky

Lasky, Kathryn. *The Man Who Made Time Travel.* Illus. Kevin Hawkes. New York: Farrar, Straus, and Giroux, 2003. Biography of John Harrison, an eighteenth century clockmaker who developed a way to find longitude at sea. (Grades 4-12)

Lasky, Kathryn. *A Brilliant Streak: The Making of Mark Twain.* Illus. Barry Moser. New York: Harcourt Brace, 1998. (Grades 4-12)

Myers, Walter Dean. *I've Seen the Promised Land: The Life of Dr. Martin Luther King, Jr.* Illus. Leonard Jenkins. New York: HarperCollins, 2004. (Grades 4-12)

Summary: Myers has teamed with illustrator Jenkins to produce a beautiful biography, outstanding among the many notable books about Dr. King, The text is eloquent, but without the overtly admiring tone of some biographies, allowing the facts to speak for themselves about Dr. King's actions and beliefs. The style of each illustration is tailored specifically to the subject of the text for that page, making the illustrations speak powerfully to the emotion of the time. There is a sense of continuity to the pictures, but the style of each stands separately in a very effective way.

Book Links: Other Notable Recent Biographies of Dr. King

Farris, Christine King. *My Brother Martin: A Sister Remembers Growing Up With the Rev. Dr. Martin Luther King, Jr.* Illus. Chris Soentpiet. New York: Simon & Schuster Books for Young Readers, 2003. (Grades 4-12)

Rappaport, Doreen. *Martin's Big Words: The Life of Dr. Martin Luther King, Jr.* Illus. Bryan Collier. New York: Hyperion Books, 2001. (Grades 4-12)

Myers, Walter Dean. *Malcolm X: A Fire Burning Brightly.* Illus. Leonard Jenkins. New York: HarperCollins, 2000. (Grades 4-12)

Summary: This book makes an interesting comparison to *I've Seen the Promised Land: the Life of Dr. Martin Luther King, Jr.* in two major ways. First, both are about major civil rights leaders, King and Malcolm X, whose lives and methods were very different. Second, the same author/illustrator team produced both books. In this book, Myers provides a simple biography of Malcolm X from childhood until his assassination. The text includes many quotations and a thorough timeline. After learning about the differences between the two civil rights leaders, students can compare the artwork Jenkins has produced for Malcolm X's story with the artwork in the biography of Dr. Martin Luther King, Jr. Did the illustrator reflect the similarities and differences in their philosophies?

Martin, Jacqueline Briggs. *Snowflake Bentley.* Illus. Mary Azarian. Boston, MA: Houghton Mifflin, 1998. (Grades 4-12)

Summary: Wilson Bentley was a self-taught scientist whose passion was photographing snowflakes. His pictures revealed to the world that no two snowflakes are alike. While his pursuit never made him rich, it enriched the science of snow, and his book, *Snow Crystals*, remains useful to scholars today. This book won the Caldecott Medal in 1998 for its beautiful, effective mix of text and art. Visit the Snowflake Bentley Museum online, <http://snowflakebentley.com/museum.htm>, for more information, pictures of snowflakes and activities.

McCully, Emily Arnold. *Pirate Queen*. New York: Putnam, 1995. (Grades 4-12)

Summary: This dashing biography of Grania O'Malley, an Irish maiden who became a fierce pirate and land baron, would be good to use in the study of English/Irish relations in the time of Queen Elizabeth I. A mixture of truth and legend, the story details Grania's rise to power in Ireland. When a ruthless English Governor, Sir Richard Bingham, crumbled the empire she had built, Grania turned to piracy as a means to fight back. Grania O'Malley went to the court of Queen Elizabeth I to petition for relief from Sir Bingham's reign. It is noteworthy that she approached the Queen as an equal rather than a conquered foe.

Pinkney, Andrea Davis. *Dear Benjamin Banneker*. Illus. Brian Pinkney. New York: Harcourt Brace, 1994. (Grades 4-12)

Summary: This brief biography of Benjamin Banneker focuses on his correspondence with, then, Secretary of State Thomas Jefferson, discussing the need for slavery to end. It is interesting to note that Banneker spoke his mind about slavery to someone in the government nearly one hundred years before the Civil War. Research topics include Benjamin Banneker, the Civil War, and protests of slavery before the Civil War. The documentation provided by personal letters is also an interesting line of study—how does the electronic communication of today affect the kinds of historical documentation future historians will have to use for research?

Book Links: Andrea Davis Pickney

Pinkney, Andrea Davis. *Duke Ellington*. Illus. Brian Pinkney. New York: Hyperion, 1997. (Grades 4-8)

Pinkney, Andrea Davis. *Ella Fitzgerald: The Tale of a Vocal Virtuoso*. Illus. Brian Pinkney. New York: Hyperion books, 2002. (Grades 4-8)

Ryan, Pam Munoz. *Amelia and Eleanor Go For a Ride*. Illus. Brian Selznick. New York: Scholastic, 1999. (Grades 4-8)

Summary: In 1932, Amelia Earhart met Eleanor Roosevelt at a function where Amelia was to give a speech, and the two women became friends. On April 20, 1933, Amelia and her husband dined with the Roosevelts at the White House. Later that evening, the two women went on a flight over Washington D. C. Ryan has fictionalized this account to show the two women flying alone. In truth, while Amelia did fly the plane for a time, regulations required two Eastern Transport pilots to man the controls. The author's note explains her deviations from the known facts for the purpose of storytelling. This account will enrich students' knowledge of both of these admirable women.

Ryan, Pam Munoz. *When Marian Sang*. Illus. Brian Selznick. New York: Scholastic, 2002. (Grades 4-12)

Summary: Marian Anderson's most famous concert was on the steps of the Lincoln Memorial for a crowd of over 75,000 people. This concert was arranged after she had been denied the opportunity to sing at Constitution Hall, which was for whites only. At the time, she was performing in halls all around the world. Her most treasured performance, however, was the day she was finally invited to sing with the Metropolitan Opera, her childhood dream come true. The book mimics the interior of the Metropolitan Opera, complete with stage, where the action unfolds. The title page is a program for the "True Recital of Marian Anderson, the Voice of the Century." A bibliography and a discography are included. Using one of the suggested discs to introduce students to Anderson's music would complement the reading of this story.

Ryan, Zoe Alderfer. *Ann and Liv Cross Antarctica: A Dream Come True*. Illus. Nicholas Reti. Cambridge, MA: Da Capo Press, 2001. (Grades 4-12)

Summary: Ann Bancroft of Minnesota and Liv Andersen of Norway dreamt separately of crossing Antarctica. This is the story of the two women, who met and discovered they shared a dream. Together, they accomplished their dream in 2001, as people all over the world watched via the Internet. Bancroft and Andersen continue to update their activities at their Web site, <http://www.yourexpedition.com/>. This adventuresome biography will motivate students to learn more about present day explorers and adventurers. Students may wish to follow the progress of other scientific expeditions, explorations, and adventures on the Internet.

Sabuda, Robert. *Tutankhamen's Gift*. New York: Atheneum, 1994. (Grades 4-8)

Summary: Young King Tut rose to power at age ten. The simplicity of the text makes this biography more suited to upper elementary and middle school, but is worth a look for students of any age for the brilliant artwork. The brightly colored illustrations are true to the historical period. When using *Tutankhamen's Gift* to study the artwork, be sure to include some of Robert Sabuda's other incredible picture books, listed in Chapter 6.

Sis, Peter. *The Tree of Life: A Book Depicting the Life of Charles Darwin*. New York: Farrar, Straus, and Giroux, 2003. (Grades 4-12)

Summary: Charles Darwin always regretted that he could not draw, so, he filled his journals with detailed descriptions. Peter Sis has scoured those journals and Darwin's publications to develop a biography of Darwin filled with detailed drawings, including journal entries as Darwin might have wanted to picture them. *The Tree of Life* covers Darwin's life from birth to death, including his education, his years on the ship *The Beagle*, and his subsequent work on natural selection. Sis divided

Darwin's life into three strands: his personal life, his public work, and his secret work. (While it eventually became public, for many years his major work on the theory of natural selection was a closely guarded secret.) This extraordinary book does not lend itself to reading aloud, but requires multiple perusals and careful study. It will raise many questions for student researchers, leading many to learn more about the life of Darwin and the theory of evolution, among other topics.

Discussion Questions:

- Charles Darwin's father objected strongly to his voyage on *The Beagle*, and listed the reasons for his opposition in a letter to Charles. How would you have answered these objections? Would you have given in and allowed your son to go on this voyage?

- Darwin wrote that he was not inclined to subscribe to the ideas of others, and that he strove to keep his mind flexible and free to change his position if his observations or new facts proved him wrong. Do you think you could do that? What if you had held an opinion about something for years and suddenly encountered facts you had not known? Would it be hard to give up your position and rethink your ideas? Can you be that flexible and still argue your position if challenged, or would it be easier to argue if you did not remain open to new facts?

Activities:

- Using the imagined journal pages as a model, have students observe an animal or plant and sketch it, then, write a description to go along with the sketch.

- Practice writing detailed descriptions. Once students have written a detailed description of something, have them trade papers and attempt to create a picture of the object from the description. Try having students describe something without naming the object, then, take turns trying to figure out what the object is from the description.

- Choose a detailed description of a setting or object from literature. Have students work in groups or alone to sketch the setting or object.

- Choose one of Darwin's journal entries from the text, and have students try to draw what he described. Students will then be able to compare their attempt with the corresponding drawing by Sis.

- Read and discuss a more lengthy biography of Darwin or an excerpt from his writing.

- Darwin wrote that he had the leisure to pursue his line of work because he did not have to earn a living, but Sis does not really tell us where his income came from. Find out how Darwin was able to afford to pursue his work, publish, own land, and raise a family.

Book Links: Peter Sis

Sis, Peter. *Tibet: Through the Red Box*. New York: Farrar Straus Giroux, 1998. (Grades 4-12)

Summary: The author's father, Vladimar Sis, was a filmmaker who journeyed to Tibet to document the construction of a highway in the 1950s. China invaded the country during his stay. He remained trapped in Tibet for two years, unable to communicate with his family or return home. Vladimar kept his journal from those years locked in a red box until 1994, when he gave it to Peter. *Tibet Through the Red Box* is the result. Use this book as a resource for students studying the Dalai Lama and Tibet, as well as for studies of art.

Sis, Peter. *Starry Messenger.* New York: Farrar, Straus, Giroux. 1996. A biography of Galileo. (Grades 4-12)

Sis, Peter. *Follow the Dream.* New York: Knopf, 1991. A biography of Columbus. (Grades 4-12)

Stanley, Diane. *Leonardo Da Vinci.* New York: Morrow, 1996. (Grades 4-12)

Summary: This history of the brilliant inventor and artist follows him from birth to death. While da Vinci was born to a noble father and raised primarily in his father's household, he was illegitimate and therefore, denied a noble profession. Art was not a noble profession, so, he became an artist's apprentice. His learning expanded into a study of the fields of anatomy, nature, science, and invention. He never became rich, but his greatest wealth was in the ideas, experiments, written entries, and drawings in his famous journals. The illustrations are in the style of the period and include reproductions of sketches from da Vinci's journals.

Discussion Questions:

- Leonardo da Vinci started many projects and paintings but did not finish them. Stanley proposed one possible reason for this. Can you think of other reasons why an artist might abandon a painting partway through?

- Stanley discusses the controversy over da Vinci's death—did he die in the arms of the King of France or not? Given the evidence the author cites, what side would you be on in the debate?

Activities:

- Possible research topics include the art of the Renaissance, da Vinci's art, the inventions of da Vinci, the political structure of Italy in this era, and the class system in Italy during the Renaissance.

- Students can examine the role the printing press played in the development of a literate society and how that may have led to the Renaissance.

- Have students read Stanley's biography of Michelangelo as a comparison to da Vinci. Discuss the similarity of the two artists' lives, the rivalry between them, and the differences in their styles.

Book Links: Diane Stanley

Stanley, Diane. *Michelangelo.* New York: HarperCollins, 2000. (Grades 4-12)

Summary: *Michelangelo* is another example of Stanley's deep research and talent in illustrating in the style of the time. This works well paired with the Leonardo da Vinci biography, as they were contemporaries. It shows, in particular, how the artists of the time were at the mercy of their patrons—many of Michelangelo's works were unfinished because the funding patron lost interest or died. It is very interesting to learn that while the fresco on the ceiling of the Sistine Chapel is one of his masterworks, Michelangelo disliked painting and did not want to take the commission.

Stanley, Diane. *Saladin: Noble Prince of Islam.* New York: HarperCollins, 2002. (Grades 4-12)

Summary: This is a biography of Saladin, who united Muslims against the third wave of Crusaders, led by Richard the Lionhearted of England. Saladin was an accomplished warrior and a generous, benevolent, principled ruler. This book helps the reader understand the background of the Crusades as well as the remarkable story of the great Muslim leader. The illustrations are in the style of Islamic art of the Middle Ages. An author's note gives a historical context to the story, and the postscript wraps up the lives of the major leaders of the various armies. A glossary and bibliography are included.

Stanley, Diane. *The True Adventures of Daniel Hall.* New York: Dial Books, 1995. (Grades 4-12)

Summary: Daniel Hall was a fourteen-year-old boy when he left home to go on a whaling voyage. His adventures included two years of whaling, during which he suffered mistreatment and abuse from the ship's captain. After deserting the ship, he lived one winter and spring in Siberia. He, then, signed onto another ship and spent another year working his way back home on various whaling ships. He wrote of his adventures in a book called *Artic Rovings.* Stanley has translated *Artic Rovings* from the stilted, formal style popular in Daniel's time into a stirring illustrated adventure story.

Stanley, Diane, and Peter Vennema. *Shaka: King of the Zulus.* New York: Morrow, 1998. (Grades 4-12)

Summary: This biography details the life of the great African leader, Shaka, who was exiled from his tribe with his mother at a young age. As a teenager, he redesigned the weapon of the Zulu, the assegai, and developed new combat techniques. He emerged as a leader of warriors and, eventually, became the King of the Zulus. While his reign lasted only ten years, he led the Zulu people from a small clan to a powerful nation with the finest warriors in Africa. His fame as a military genius is worldwide. Stanley has included a bibliography and a pronunciation guide.

Stanley, Diane, and Peter Vennema. *Bard of Avon: The Story of William Shakespeare.* New York: Morrow, 1992. (Grades 4-12)

Stanley, Diane, and Peter Vennema. *Charles Dickens: The Man Who Had Great Expectations.* New York: Morrow, 1993. (Grades 4-12)

Stanley, Diane, and Peter Vennema. *Cleopatra.* New York: Morrow, 1994. (Grades 4-12)

Stanley, Diane, and Peter Vennema. *Good Queen Bess: The Story of Elizabeth I of England.* Illus. Diane Stanley. New York: HarperCollins, 1990. (Grades 4-12)

Stanley, Diane. *Joan of Arc*. New York: Morrow, 1998. (Grades 4-12)

Stanley, Diane. *Peter the Great*. New York: Four Winds Press, 1986. (Grades 4-12)

Walker, Alice. *Langston Hughes: American Poet*. Illus. Catherine Deeter. New York: HarperCollins, 2002. (Grades 4-12)

Summary: Alice Walker, author of *The Color Purple*, wrote this biography of Langston Hughes, hoping to lead children to his poetry. As a child, Hughes learned many lessons from those around him. He discovered that there are many varieties of racism, but that the color of your skin made the biggest difference in being able to get a job. His father became a rich man in Mexico, and while Langston never lived with his father, he got to know him well. He realized that his father hated blacks and put himself above the majority of black people. Langston lived most of his childhood with his grandmother, who old him true stories about his grandfather fighting to free slaves. He loved New York City, and spent many years living in and around Harlem. He wrote his first poem at the age of fourteen, and continued to write all of his life.

Chapter 6

Art and Poetry in Picture Books

The illustrations in picture books interact with the story, making the whole greater than the two parts. The role of art in picture books can be simply to illustrate the story, but the best picture books are a meld of both story and pictures. In addition, picture books are the first opportunity for many children to see and appreciate different kinds of art. Contemporary picture book illustrators use many different media and techniques to create the art for picture books. This gives readers access to a huge variety of art forms. In that sense, many picture books are worthy of study for the art contained within. Some of the annotations in previous chapters of this book have included ideas about using the artwork or style for art lessons or appreciation.

The Caldecott Medal, named for children's book illustrator Randolph Caldecott, honors illustrators of the "most distinguished American picture book for children." These selections always do an excellent job of blending text and pictures to the greatest advantage. The lists of winners and honor books, found at <http://www.ala.org/ala/alsc/awardsscholarships/literaryawds/caldecottmedal/caldecottmedal.htm>, are a great resource for some of the best artwork in children's literature.

One excellent use for picture books is to look at how different artists interpret the same text. For example, several illustrated versions of Longfellow's poem "The Midnight Ride of Paul Revere" are currently available. Students will be able to compare and contrast the versions to see how the various artists chose to portray the characters, action, and landscape in each book.

Sometimes, the design of a book stretches the boundaries of picture books. Illustrators and designers are using the end papers, the title, and dedication pages to extend the text and pictures in unusual ways. For the *Dinosaurs of Waterhouse Hawkins* and *When Marian Sang*, the design of the book itself makes an artistic statement along with the book and illustrations. *When Marian Sang* (annotated in Chapter 5) opens with the reader seated in the audience looking at the program for the concert. The curtains part and the story begins. *The Dinosaurs of Waterhouse Hawkins* begins with a stage and play bill for a "True Dinosaur Story in Three Ages" and ends with the menu for the dinner party pictured in the book.

In a number of picture books, art is the main focus. Thomas Locker's books are poetic, but the art takes center stage. While his books are lyrical and contribute knowledge in content areas, such as science, Locker's books provide good examples of landscape painting and the artist taking cues from nature.

Poetry is another art form contained in picture books. Art and poetry seem naturally suited to one another and combine effectively in many books. One can see many examples of this happy combination in picture books. Picture books illustrating a single poem are suitable for use in discussions of interpretation of poems. Short, illustrated collections of poetry are useful in introducing poetry in many ways. Some collections feature the work of a specific poet, while others combine poems on a single topic by various poets. Many picture books feature one style, such as haiku, throughout the book, or, as in *Leap into Poetry*, highlight a different style of poetry on each page.

The picture books in this chapter are a small sample of what is available. Artists whose vehicles are picture books are many and varied. A librarian or teacher will find examples of many art media and techniques in the world of picture books. Since picture books rely on art, it is easy to find books that will promote activities focusing on the art. Books in this chapter will support poetry, writing, literature, or art classes, but many also have value in science and history units. Once librarians begin looking at the art and poetry in picture books, many other ideas will present themselves.

 ## Books about Artists

Lasky, Kathryn. *First Painter*. Illus. Rocco Baviera. New York: DK, 2000. (Grades 4-12)

Summary: *First Painter* tells the story of Mishoo, a girl in prehistoric times. She is the daughter of her tribe's Dream Catcher. When her mother dies, she must become the new Dream Catcher. The tribe is enduring a three-year drought, and Mishoo must find a way to bring the rain through her dreams. She is unsuccessful until she heeds the dreams that tell her to go to the tiger's cave. In the cave, she becomes an artist, drawing on the walls. The artist has used authentic materials and pigments to mix the paints to make this book as true to the time as possible.

Discussion Questions:

- The author says this is an "imaginative reconstruction of the birth of the artistic imagination." What is artistic imagination? Find examples of artistic imagination in the text to support your answers. Can anyone have that kind of imagination?

- Mishoo painted many legs on the horses to show movement. What are other ways to show movement in pictures?

- Have you ever looked at a rock or tree and seen shapes that reminded you of other things?

Activities:

- Find pictures of cave paintings. Titles such as *Mystery of the Lascaux Cave* by Dorothy Hinshaw Patent, and *The Cave of Lascaux: The Final Photographs* by Mario Ruspoli may be helpful. Students can search the Internet for current Web sites regarding cave paintings. Compare the ancient cave art to Mishoo's paintings and to the illustrator's style.

- Have students try to make a painting in the style of cave painters.

- Many of the cave paintings seem to tell a story. Find a picture from a cave and have students write the story they see in the painting.

Ancona, George. *Murals: Walls that Sing.* New York: Marshall Cavendish, 2003. (Grades 4-12)

Summary: George Ancona is a photojournalist who has published several books for children. In this book, he features and celebrates outdoor murals from around the world. They range from ancient cave paintings to murals by individual artists and community efforts. The art styles vary widely, and include graffiti, iconic paintings, and children's art. The text guides us through this tour of murals, explaining the construction methods, historical contexts, and purposes of each artwork. This book provides some background and ideas for students who are planning a mural. Art classes may study the book for ideas and motivation for murals.

Book Links: Murals

Knight, Margy Burns. *Talking Walls.* Illus. Anne Sibley O'Brien. Gardiner, ME: Tilbury House, 1992. (Grades 4-12)

Knight, Margy Burns *Talking Walls: The Stories Continue.* Illus. Anne Sibley O'Brien. Gardiner, ME: Tilbury House, 1996. (Grades 4-12)

Kerley, Barbara. *The Dinosaurs of Waterhouse Hawkins: An Illuminating History of Mr. Waterhouse Hawkins, Artist and Lecturer.* Illus. Brian Selznick. New York: Scholastic, 2001. (Grades 4-12)

Summary: Waterhouse Hawkins was a Victorian artist who dreamed of making models of dinosaurs. This book shows his artistry, his quest for scientific information, his bold risk taking and ultimately, his frustrations and failures. Hawkins was successful in making the first models of dinosaurs, and was two years into a project for a Paleozoic Museum in Central Park when William "Boss" Tweed, a corrupt but powerful New York politician, put an end to the museum and Hawkins's dreams. Endnotes give more information. Selznick uses several styles and palettes to illustrate this book, which was a Caldecott Honor book for 2002.

Books featuring Art

Locker, Thomas, and Candace Christiansen. *Sky Tree*. New York: HarperCollins, 1995. (Grades 4-12)

Summary: For *Sky Tree*, Locker painted the same scene, a tree on a knoll by a river, fourteen times. The paintings portray different seasons and times of day. The text is poetic, describing briefly the activity of nature in and around the tree. At the bottom of each page is a question about the painting to encourage contemplation and discussion. At the end of the book, thumbnails accompany the questions and possible answers.

Activities:

- Consider and discuss the questions with your students. Compare the discussion at the back of the book with your ideas. This is an excellent medium for learning that there is no single right answer for every question.

- Use one of the paintings as a story starter or inspiration for a poem. If possible, make a color transparency of the page to place on an overhead projector, or scan the picture into your computer to project it so your students can see the painting better.

- Have students create their own sky tree painting or drawing. The medium used will vary with the age of the student and your objective. Students could draw the tree one time in a particular season or make a four-part picture showing the same scene in four seasons. For a similar concept from a historical perspective, see *A Street Through Time* by Anne Millard, annotated in Chapter 4.

Book Links: Thomas Locker

Locker, Thomas. *Mountain Dance*. San Diego, CA: Harcourt, 2001. (Grades 4-12)

Summary: Locker's signature oil paintings and lyrical text illuminate types of mountains. Locker's focus in this book is the geological history of the formation of mountains—how the forces of nature shape them. The more detailed information at the back of the book includes thumbnail sized reproductions of the pictures.

Locker, Thomas. *Cloud Dance*. San Diego, CA: Harcourt, 2000. (Grades 4-12)

Summary: Locker's text begins, "In every time and season/ the colors of clouds/ are always changing." He, then, presents fourteen paintings featuring clouds in many forms and seasons, each accompanied by one poetic sentence. A page of information is included along with a very useful one-page illustration showing the different types of clouds. The formations would never be in the sky all at once as in this picture, but it provides an extremely handy way to learn their names and shapes.

Gonsalves, Rob, and Sarah L. Thompson. *Imagine a Night*. Illus. Rob Gonsalves. New York: Atheneum, 2003. (Grades 4-12)

Summary: Gonsalves's paintings are like luminous, magical dreamscapes. In every painting, the landscape changes and can be seen two ways. For instance, the cover art shows a nighttime scene of a lake surrounded by forest. The reflections of the trees in the lake become a series of ghostly women walking out of the lake up onto the shore. It is as if Escher and Van Allsburg combined their artistic ideas and styles. The focus in this book is on the paintings, but Sarah Thompson has added a small amount of text to go with each picture. Each page begins with "Imagine a night..." and gives just a few poetic words inspired by the painting. With or without the text, these paintings set imagination in motion.

Discussion Questions:

- For any of the paintings in the book, these questions arise: What was the artist thinking? What does this mean? What is your interpretation of this scene? What is real and what is imaginary?

- Is this artist seeing the world differently than others, or is he inventing a world of his own?

Activities:

- Use these paintings as story starters. Put the picture up for the students to see without the text, and have them write the story behind the picture. These pictures lend themselves to flights of fancy, but the format of the writing could be poetry or prose. A teacher could assign a paragraph, a poem, or a story.

- Students can try to draw this kind of picture, where one reality seems to blend into another. More examples of Gonsalves's paintings are on the Internet (for sale), at <http://www.progressiveart.com/gonsalves_page.htm>.

- Have students research M. C. Escher and compare his work with Gonsalves's. The 1983 poster book, *M.C. Escher, 29 Master Prints* will give students a representation of his work, and there are several detailed books of Escher's work for further study.

Van Allsburg, Chris. *The Mysteries of Harris Burdick*. Boston: Houghton Mifflin, 1984. (Grades 4-12)

Summary: While many of Chris Van Allsburg's books are suitable for use with older readers, and many contain mysterious pictures, this title is the best comparison with Gonsalves's *Imagine a Night*. The black and white pictures depict mysterious scenes accompanied by a title and brief caption that deepen the mystery. These are intriguing story starters by themselves and will be useful in comparisons with Gonsalves's work.

Davol, Marguerite W. *The Paper Dragon*. Illus. Robert Sabuda. New York: Atheneum, 1997. (Grades 4-12)

Summary: Mi Fei is a humble scroll painter sent by his village to confront the dragon Sui Jen, who is ravaging the countryside. He must convince the dragon to return to its hundred years' sleep. The dragon gives him three seemingly impossible tasks. In each case, Mi Fei beats the dragon with his wit and his art. Fold out pages illustrate the problems and the artist's solutions. To create the pictures, Sabuda painted tissue paper, cut shapes, and placed them on Japanese handmade Sugikawashi paper. The resulting illustrations are beautiful and intricate, and resemble scrolls.

Activities:

- Collect several picture books illustrated with collage to compare and contrast. See the book links for suggested titles. Many collage illustrators make their own paper or purchase handmade paper, and use many different kinds of paints. Students can examine the variety of collage techniques and research the methods used by the different artists. Choose one form of collage for students to use to make a picture. *The Art of Paper Collage*, by Susan Pickering Rothamel, covers many techniques, and *Making Collages*, by Susan Johnston, provides instructions for beginners.

- Experiment with creating handmade paper. *Papermaking*, by Claudia Lee, includes instructions for making paper, plus, projects using your new paper. *Papermaking Techniques*, by John Plowman, gives directions for 50 different methods of making paper.

- Paper engineering, the art of pop-ups, is fascinating to students. Gather several pop-up books to serve as examples, and have students create pop-up illustrations. *The Usborne Book of Pop-Ups*, by Richard Dungworth, and *How to Make Super Pop-Ups*, by Joan Irvine, will help students learn the mechanics of paper engineering.

- Sabuda illustrates books using many media, including collage, painted glass, and pop-up books. Any of his books can serve as inspiration to try a new technique. The following Book Links list the medium in parentheses at the end of the citation.

Book Links: Robert Sabuda

Sabuda, Robert. *The Blizzard's Robe*. New York: Atheneum Books for Young Readers, 1999. (Grades 4-12) (Batik)

Sabuda, Robert. *Saint Valentine*. New York: Atheneum, 1992. (Grades 4-12) (Paper mosaics)

Sabuda, Robert. *Arthur and the Sword*. New York: Atheneum Books for Young Readers, 1995. (Grades 4-12) (Stained glass style painted on glass)

Sabuda, Robert. *The Movable Mother Goose*, New York: Little Simon, 1999. (Grades 4-12) (Pop-up)

Sabuda, Robert. *The Christmas Alphabet*. New York: Orchard Books, 1994. (Grades 4-12) (Pop-up)

Sabuda, Robert. *Tutankhamen's Gift*. New York: Atheneum, 1994. (Grades 4-12) (Cut paper and ink on papyrus)

Book Links: Collage

Carle, Eric. *Dream Snow*. New York: Philomel Books, 2000. (Grades 4-12)

Carle, Eric. *Mr. Seahorse*. New York: Philomel Books, 2004. (Grades 4-12)

Ehlert, Lois. *Market Day: a Story Told with Folk Art*. San Diego: Harcourt, 2000. (Grades 4-12)

Ehlert, Lois. *Pie in the Sky*. Orlando, FL: Harcourt, 2004. (Grades 4-12)

Jenkins, Steve. *Actual Size*. Boston, MA: Houghton Mifflin, 2004. (Grades 4-12)

Jenkins, Steve. *Hottest, Coldest, Highest, Deepest*. Boston, MA: Houghton Mifflin, 2004. (Grades 4-12)

Fleming, Denise. *Buster*. New York: Henry Holt, 2003. (Grades 4-12)

Fleming, Denise. *Pumpkin Eye*. New York: Henry Holt, 2001. (Grades 4-12)

Art and Poetry—Books with One Poem

Angelou, Maya. *Life Doesn't Frighten Me*. Illus. Jean-Michel Basquiat. New York: Stewart, Tabori, and Chang, 1993. (Grades 4-12)

Summary: Angelou's poem "Life Doesn't Frighten Me" appears in a stark font, white on black and black on white, with bold, provocative, modern illustrations by Jean-Michel Basquiat. This serves as a good introduction to the poet and the artist. Two-page biographies of both the poet and the artist are included in the back of the book. The biography of Basquiat tells of his development from a graffiti artist to a world-renowned painter who has been compared to Pablo Picasso, Willem de Kooning, Jasper Johns, and Jean Dubuffet. It mentions his early death from an accidental drug overdose at the age of twenty-seven. There is much fodder for discussion here, especially with teenagers.

Discussion Questions:

- What does the poet mean when she writes, "Life doesn't frighten me?" Can life be frightening? What is frightening to you?

- How do the illustrations give you ideas of the things that frighten the artist?

Activities:

- Read the poem to the students without showing the book or illustrations. Put the text of the poem on the overhead and have students respond to it in writing or by drawing. Discuss any questions the poem raises for students. Read the book a second time, sharing Basquiat's illustrations. Ask students how the art has changed or added to their perceptions of the poem, and what they thought of the art.

- Pick one of the things that Angelou says does not frighten her, and write a response to it. Does she really mean that she is not frightened? Are there other things that could be added to her poem—things that are extremely scary about modern life?

- Research the life of Jean-Michel Basquiat. Develop questions from the biography at the end of the book to guide your research. The film entitled *Basquiat* will provide more information.

Longfellow, Henry Wadsworth. *The Song of Hiawatha.* Illus. Margaret Early. Brooklyn, New York: Handprint Books, 2003. (Grades 4-12)

Summary: Margaret Early has illustrated selections from the epic poem of Hiawatha. Each excerpt links to the next with brief text explaining what happens between the two pieces. Intricately designed frames border the beautiful illustrations and text . This book has many possible uses: to add a visual arts dimension to the study of the full-length poem, as an introduction to Longfellow or the poem "Hiawatha," or as a study of the artistic style.

Longfellow, Henry Wadsworth. *The Midnight Ride of Paul Revere.* Illus. Christopher Bing. New York: Handprint Books, 2001. (Grades 4-12)

Longfellow, Henry Wadsworth. *The Midnight Ride of Paul Revere.* Illus. Jeffrey Thompson. Washington DC: National Geographic Society, 1999. (Grades 4-12)

Longfellow, Henry Wadsworth. *Paul Revere's Ride.* Illus. Ted Rand. New York: Dutton Children's Books, 1990. (Grades 4-12)

Longfellow, Henry Wadsworth. *Paul Revere's Ride.* Illus. Nancy Winslow Parker. New York: Greenwillow Books, 1985. (Grades 4-12)

Summary: These four renditions of "The Midnight Ride of Paul Revere" are very different in style and art. Use two or more of the versions as a compare and contrast lesson in the way artists view the same text differently. The Bing version contains additional information about the times, maps detailing the British campaign, and replicas of important documents. Some of the documents attach to pages of the book as foldout extras. The other three versions are simply illustrations of the poem without additional historical information.

Noyes, Alfred. *The Highwayman.* Illus. Neil Waldman. New York: Harcourt Brace, 1990. (Grades 4-12)

Summary: This famous romantic poem by Alfred Noyes tells the story of Bess, the innkeeper's daughter, and her true love, the highwayman. When King George's soldiers use Bess as bait to catch the highwayman, she finds a way to warn her lover, saving his life at the expense of her own. In the tradition of romantic tragedy, he learns of her sacrifice and rushes to a deadly encounter with the soldiers. Waldman's watercolor illustrations show the highwayman in shadow and silhouette.

Burleigh, Robert. *Hoops*. Illus. Stephen T. Johnson. New York, Harcourt Brace, 1997. (Grades 4-12)

Summary: Burleigh's poem describes the sounds, sights, textures, smells, and emotions of playing basketball. Short, punchy lines and dynamic painting give a sense of the movement of the game. The illustrations provide snapshots of players in action on an outdoor court. Use *Hoops* as an example of free verse.

Book Links: Art and Poetry—Books with One Poem

Frost, Robert. *Stopping by Woods on a Snowy Evening*. Illus. Susan Jeffers. New York, Dutton, 1978. (Grades 4-12)

Myers, Christopher. *Black Cat*. New York: Scholastic, 1999. (Grades 4-12)

Myers, Christopher. *Blues Journey*. New York: Holiday House, 2003. (Grades 4-12)

Myers, Walter Dean. *Harlem*. Illus. Christopher Myers. New York: Scholastic, 1997. (Grades 4-12)

Willard, Nancy. *Pish, Posh, Said Hieronymus Bosch*. Illus. Leo and Diane Dillon. New York: Harcourt Brace, 1991. (Grades 4-12)

Art and Poetry—Picture Books with Collections of Poetry

Whipple, Laura. *If the Shoe Fits: Voices From Cinderella*. Illus. Laura Beingessner. New York: Margaret K. McElderry, 2002. (Grades 7-12)

Summary: This collection of poems tells the Cinderella story from the perspectives of all the characters involved, beginning with the ghost of Cinderella's father and including the wicked stepmother, the prince, the guests at the ball, and even the glass slippers and Cinderella's housecat! The poems move the story forward, revisiting each character in turn. The thoughts and feelings in this book run deep, and students below seventh grade may not grasp the meaning. High school students will bring the most understanding to this text.

Activities:

- Read *If the Shoe Fits* aloud. Pause between poems for discussion of the thoughts and feelings contained in each poem. Students will bring their own questions into the discussion.

- Many of the characters in the story narrate more than one poem. Have students, in small groups, examine the poems from one of the characters. Each group can take a different character and list characteristics, feelings, and actions of that character.

- Choose another fairy tale and work in groups to create poems from the point of view of each character in the story. Put the poems together to make a whole story. How does it change students' thinking to consider the point of view of all of the characters?

- Many novels use a similar device—different characters are speaking in different chapters or each chapter includes pieces from each of the main characters' point of view. Reading this story where the poems clearly demonstrate different points of view may help students comprehend the strategy when used in a larger piece of writing, such as a novel.

Greenberg, Jan, Ed. *Heart to Heart: New Poems Inspired by Twentieth-Century American Art.* New York: Abrams, 2001. (Grades 4-12)

Summary: For this lengthy picture book collection, Greenberg invited contemporary American poets to choose a twentieth-century American work of art and write a poem inspired by the artwork. The poems, accompanied by reproductions of the art, are divided into four chapters by motif; Stories, Voices, Impressions, and Expressions. Biographical notes on both poets and artists and an index make the book extremely useful for teachers and librarians. The discussion questions that follow can be used with any of the selections.

Discussion Questions:

- Was the poet successful in expressing the meaning the artist was trying to convey?

- Did the poem fit with your perception of the artwork? Could people have different ideas about the meaning of a piece of art?

Activities:

- With such a variety of poetry and art, students will be sure to find one poet or artist interesting enough to investigate. Research could be as simple as finding other works by the same artist or as complicated as a full research report on an artist or poet.

- After sharing some of the poems, show students one of the pictures and ask them to write a poem in response to the art. Discuss the differences and similarities between the students' poems and the published poem.

- Choose a piece of art not included in *Heart to Heart*, and have students write a poem or prose inspired by that art.

Feelings, Tom. *Soul Looks Back in Wonder.* New York: Dial, 1993. (Grades 4-12)

Summary: Artist Tom Feelings asked thirteen African American poets to contribute to this collection. It is interesting to note that Feeling chose the paintings for this book and, then, selected poems to fit with the paintings. In contrast to *Heart to Heart*, only one of the poems is a direct response to the painting written especially for this book. Discuss with students how this changes their thoughts about the paintings and the poetry. Does it matter who selected the poems? Why would the artist not ask the poets to write especially for the pictures?

Janeczko, Paul. *A Poke in the I: A Collection of Concrete Poems*. Illus. Chris Raschka. Cambridge, MA: Candlewick Press, 2001. (Grades 4-12)

Summary: Thirty concrete poems with lively illustrations by Raschka make this book a visual delight. The title poem in this clever collection resembles an eye chart, with ever decreasing font size: "I/ NEED/ CONTACT/ LENSES/ like I need a poke in the eye." Use *A Poke in the I* to introduce a lesson on concrete poetry. For more examples of concrete poetry in picture book format, see *Flicker Flash* by Joan Bransfield Graham.

Harley, Avis. *Fly With Poetry: An ABC of Poetry*. Honesdale, PA: Wordsong/Boyds Mills Press, 2000. (Grades 4-12)

Harley, Avis. *Leap into Poetry: More ABCs of Poetry*. Honesdale, PA: Wordsong/Boyds Mills Press, 2001. (Grades 4-12)

Summary: Each page of these two volumes features a different type of poem. The author has included a brief definition of each form. While the author states that these are not how-to guides for writing poetry, teachers and librarians will be able to glean many wonderful ideas for poetry lessons from them. Just the sheer variety of poetry and word play here provide a wealth of ideas and information.

Fleischman, Paul. *I Am Phoenix: Poems for Two Voices*. Illus. Ken Nutt. New York: Harper Trophy, 1985. (Grades 4-12)

Fleischman, Paul. *Joyful Noise: Poems for Two Voices*. Illus. Eric Beddows. New York: Harper and Row, 1988. (Grades 4-12)

Fleischman, Paul. *Big Talk: Poems for Four Voices*. Illus. Seppe Gicobbe. Cambridge, MA: Candlewick Press, 2000. (Grades 4-12)

Summary: Each of these books contains a group of poems made for performance. *I Am Phoenix* and *Joyful Noise* contain poems about nature; the former about birds, and the latter relating to insects. The poems in *Joyful Noise* describe insects but also try to imitate the sounds of insects when read aloud. While the books are not lavishly illustrated, they are included here as a good example of choral reading and unique placement of text on the page. The poems, graphically organized on the page so each reader knows his part, contain lines read by one person or the other, and some read by both readers. In *Big Voices*, the parts are color-coded. There are three poems in *Big Voices*, each a bit more difficult to perform. The second poem, "Seventh Grade Soap Opera" will resonate with all middle and high school students. These poems are great fun to do as choral readings, splitting a group into the appropriate number of parts. Students may be more willing to perform their own poetry in a "Poetry Slam" format after practicing these poems together.

Waldman, Neil. *Dream Makers: Young People Share Their Hopes and Aspirations.* Honesdale, PA: Boyds Mills Press, 2003. (Grades 4-12)

Summary: The Children's Aid Society provides a wide range of programs for over 120,000 children in New York City. In honor of the society's 150-year anniversary, Neil Waldman asked young students around the United States to write about their dreams. Waldman illustrated 44 of the entries, both prose and poetry, for *Dream Makers*. The Children's Aid Society posted the remaining entries on their Web page at <www.childrensaidsociety.org/dreammakers>. *Dream Makers* will provide additional inspiration for assignments based on Martin Luther King's "I Have a Dream" speech.

Hovey, Kate. *Ancient Voices.* Illus. Murray Kimber. New York: Margaret K. McElderry Books, 2004. (Grades 4-12)

Summary: The Greek and Roman Gods tell their stories in these original poems by Hovey. Each chapter is set in a different mythical place: Mount Olympus, The Sea, The Underworld, and The Forest. The voices include Zeus, Ganymede, Hera, Poseidon, Aphrodite, Persephone, Apollo, and Diana. Appendixes give more information about the major characters and settings.

Tennyson, Alfred. *Alfred, Lord Tennyson.* Ed. John Maynard. Illus. Allen Garns. New York: Sterling, 2003. (Grades 4-12)

Williams, William Carlos. *William Carlos Williams.* Ed. Christopher MacGowan. Illus. Robert Crockett. New York: Sterling, 2004. (Grades 4-12)

Yeats, William Butler. *William Butler Yeats.* Ed. Jonathan Allison. Illus. Glenn Harrington. New York: Sterling, 2002. (Grades 4-12)

Summary: This series of picture books attempts to introduce famous poets to children. Each book contains a section telling about the featured person's life, influences, and poetry. The rest of the book consists of poems and excerpts that give the reader a taste of the work of the poet. The selections include some of the most accessible poems written by these important writers. Each two-page spread features one poem, accompanied by an illustration and brief definitions of unusual or difficult words. The editors and illustrators vary, so, each book has an individual feel and character, much like each of the poets. Librarians can read aloud from the books to give students a small sample of the poets' work. Teachers may wish to use these picture books when embarking on a more in depth study of a specific writer. Other books in the series feature Emily Dickinson, Walt Whitman, Carl Sandburg, Edna St. Vincent Millay, William Shakespeare, Robert Louis Stevenson, Robert Browning, Edward Lear, and Lewis Carroll.

Book Links: Picture Books with Collections of Poetry

Hopkins, Lee Bennett. *Home to Me: Poems Across America*. Illus. Stephen Alcorn. New York: Orchard, 2002. (Grades 4-12)

Florain, Douglas. *Insectlopedia*. San Diego, CA: Harcourt Brace, 1998. (Grades 4-12)

Begay, Shonto. *Navajo: Visions and Voices across the Mesa*. New York: Scholastic, 1995. (Grades 4-12)

Nye, Naomi Shihab. *Come With Me: Poems for a Journey*. Illus. Dan Yaccarino. New York: Greenwillow, 2000. (Grades 4-12)

Chapter 7

Go Forth and

Use Picture Books!

Picture books are a valuable tool for teachers and librarians to use with students of all ages. The ability to introduce a new topic in a succinct format is very helpful in today's sound bite world, and, often, the introduction will lead students to further research and learning. In addition, the amount of information crammed into these slim volumes is quite astounding, and even adults find new information about familiar topics in the pages of picture books. Between the deliciously "gross" facts and the "Wow—I didn't know that!" response, many current science picture books will inspire students and teachers alike.

Perhaps, the most important function of picture books is the emotional content. This is especially evident in the fields of history, poetry, and art. When students' emotions are involved, the lessons are more memorable, and the level of understanding is broader and deeper. Picture books are like the stories your grandfather told you—they made the world in his time more personal and real to you. Using these stories can add a completely new dimension to any unit. A university student recently wrote me in response to the reading she did for one of my graduate courses. She commented that many of the picture books she read for the class made her cry. It is unlikely that she will forget the stories that brought tears, and she already plans to use those books with her students.

Librarians, I urge you to find picture books that fit the curriculum, purchase them for the school library, and promote their use with teachers and administration. Read these versatile books to students, and collaborate with teachers to add the best picture books to existing units. Teachers, talk to your librarian about picture books appropriate for your grade level and curriculum. Experiment with the titles listed in *Speak to Their Hearts*, and scour libraries and bookstores to find other wonderful titles to add to the books featured here. Go forth and read!

Index of Authors and Illustrators

Index of Titles

Bibliography

Benedict, Susan, and Lenore Carlisle, Ed. *Beyond Words: Picture Books for Older Readers and Writers.* Portsmouth, NH: Heinemann, 1992.

Horning, Kathleen T. *From Cover to Cover: Evaluating and Reviewing Children's Books.* New York: HarperCollins, 1997.

Marantz, Sylvia, and Kenneth. *Multicultural Picture Books: Art for Understanding Others.* Worthington, OH: Linworth Publishing, 1994.

Marantz, Sylvia, and Kenneth. *Multicultural Picture Books: Art for Understanding Others, Volume II.* Worthington, OH: Linworth Publishing, 1997.

Saunders, Sheryl Lee. *Look—and Learn.* Portsmouth, NH: Heinemann, 1999.

About the Author

Molly Blake Pearson has been teaching in the Lakewood School District in Washington State for over twenty-six years. She has experience teaching from Kindergarten through Sixth Grade, both as a classroom teacher and a librarian. Since 1990, she has been the librarian for grades Kindergarten through Six, currently at English Crossing Elementary School, a grade Three through Five school. Molly also teaches distance-learning courses for Seattle Pacific University in the fields of Children's Literature, Reading, and Research projects for children. In 1997, she received the Christa McAuliffe Excellence in Education Award. Molly lives with her husband in Stanwood, Washington. This is her first book.